W9-CPG-804

LIBRARIES, COALITIONS & THE PUBLIC GOOD

Edited
with a Preface
and Introduction by

E. J. Josey

Neal-Schuman Publishers, Inc.

New York   London

Published by Neal-Schuman Publishers, Inc.
23 Leonard Street
New York, NY 10013

Printed and bound in the United States of America.

Library of Congress Cataloging-in-Publication Data

Libraries, coalitions, and the public good.

    Includes index.
    1. Libraries and society.   2. Libraries and community.
3. Public libraries.   4. Coalition (Social sciences).
I. Josey, E. J.
Z716.4.L47   1987   021   87-1642
ISBN 1-55570-017-9

*Dedicated with affection and appreciation
to the first librarian in my life, my high
school librarian, Margaret Jackson Bond,
who contributed enormously to the
education of the students at I. C. Norcom
High School, Portsmouth, Virginia*

Contents

Preface

E. J. Josey

Libraries, Coalitions, and the Public Good presents sixteen original papers on critical issues related to the meaning of the public good; libraries as a public good; the economic impact of libraries on American society; and the development of coalitions between libraries, educational institutions, and other organizations to meet society's needs. Most of these papers were commissioned for the 1985 American Library Association Presidential Program and comprise position papers which served as background for program participants, papers presented at the January 1985 ALA Conference, and speeches presented at ALA's annual conference, held on July 8, 1985.

The theme for the program emerged from ALA's recognition that the capacity of libraries to serve the public good is being seriously threatened by forces in American society which believe that federal funds should not be used to support certain domestic programs, including libraries.

Our goals were to explore and reaffirm the concept of the public good and to develop coalitions to foster public support for libraries and other services which contribute to the general welfare. To accomplish this goal, a day-long "conference within a conference" was organized to allow librarians, library trustees, library advocates, as well as representatives from a variety of national organizations, to engage in extensive discussions of the meaning of the public good and the role that coalitions can play in translating this concept into action. Representatives of more than fifty of the nation's leading organizations and over 1,500 librarians attended.

Libraries, Coalitions, and the Public Good is arranged in three parts followed by an Afterword. Part One, "Libraries and the

Public Good," begins with an essay by John N. Berry III entitled "The Public Good: What Is It?" Berry reviews the classic economic definition of the public good and takes issue with the views of those economists who claim that libraries do not qualify as "public goods" and are not worthy of public funding. In his formidable defense of libraries as a public good, Berry argues that, in their promotion of the general welfare, libraries fulfill the original promise upon which our nation was founded. "The people have supported libraries from their beginnings . . . based on our knowledge as citizens, that to govern ourselves, we must be informed."

"The Library's Commitment to the Public Sector," by Fay M. Blake is the topic of the second essay. Blake defines the public good as "the welfare and quality of life of *all* of us throughout the globe . . . the constituency of the public sector is precisely that portion of the population which has not made it—the poor and the disregarded." Blake states that the difficult task now facing librarians is to broaden the ideals embodied in the concept of the public good by dedicating themselves to the poor. "This may make our work more difficult," she acknowledges, but it will also "renew a sense of fulfillment for librarians within their own profession."

Virginia Ann Hodgkinson's essay, "The Public Good: The Independent Sector's Point of View," reminds us that the independent sector preceded formal government in America's history. Hodgkinson describes the independent sector as a "network of networks," a coalition of organizations working together toward preserving, giving, volunteering. This sector, she says, exemplifies democratic values and maintains our individual freedoms. In her exploration of how the independent sector has served American life, she exalts "the capacity of Americans to band together to engage in activities to serve the public good, [which] is the essence of the independent sector and, perhaps, one of the most distinctive features of American society."

In Arthur Curley's "Towards a Broader Definition of the Public Good, he urges us to link the goals and concerns of libraries with those of the American people. "We need to bypass semantic obstacles and develop a consensus and a focus . . . through which to integrate the activities of libraries with the public interest." His comments on the relationship between libraries and the free flow of information are instructive: "The free flow of information is of importance not just to libraries, but also to the broad range of other organizations to which we must turn in attempting to build coalitions."

Part One ends with an essay by Virginia Hamilton, entitled "The Library's Role in a Multicultural Society." She describes her career as a novelist and as a biographer of blacklisted minority leaders such as Dr. W.E.B. Du Bois and the great singer and actor Paul Robeson, and explains the difficulties that researchers encounter in obtaining access to full documentation of their ethnic and cultural history. Hamilton does not allow us to forget that libraries have the primary responsibility for preserving our cultural record, and she deplores the efforts of censors and current maneuvers by government officials to restrict the free flow of information.

Part Two focuses on issues that further illuminate the concept of the public good. The lead-off essay in this section, "The Awesome Mission of Library Leadership in America," was written by the Honorable Major R. Owens, the only librarian-member of the United States Congress. In his advice to the library profession, the Congressman points to pressures from government and the marketplace which threaten the integrity of libraries. "In this age of information, when new perceptions of the power of information are escalating, the business of library and information services has been perceived as too critical to be left to the library profession by itself." Owens believes that "the success of our library leadership is very much dependent on the ability of that leadership to stimulate, inspire, and unite the rest of us." In addition to forging coalitions, Owens advises us to create solidarity among all those who carry the title of librarian.

Gordon M. Ambach addresses a key issue of the conference, "The Library's Role in Supporting the Economic Health of the Nation." He alerts us to the changing nature of the work force and the work place. "In the twenty-first century, a relatively smaller work force, including a proportionally larger component of racial and ethnic minorities, will have to support the needs of a relatively larger elderly/retired population." Ambach goes on to summarize a variety of educational and job-training programs that anticipate these circumstances, and the role that libraries have played in implementing them in New York State.

Mary Hatwood Futrell addresses the topic of "Library Services to Minorities." Futrell describes the difficulties she had as a young black woman in gaining adequate and equal access to the diversity of resources in her public library. She relates her experience to the current situation in America today. "Many communities, and too many schools, lack well-equipped, well-staffed libraries to serve their public. My personal experience convinces me that in the years ahead we must make sure that our library doors swing open to all Americans."

In "Pay Equity and the Public Good," Winn Newman rejects the argument that a job's true worth cannot be determined, and that it is therefore impossible to determine an appropriate salary level within a job category. He answers: "Employers regularly measure job values, and set pay rates accordingly. The only problem is they apply different standards to women's jobs and men's jobs, and that is precisely what the law prohibits." Newman concludes his essay by asserting that what is needed to counter wage discrimination is a carefully planned litigation strategy.

Gerald R. Shields, in "The Economic Impact of Libraries," discusses the tensions inherent in any discussion of the economic contribution of libraries: Can their economic impact be measured by precise economic data? Is it desirable to view libraries in terms of their quantitative value? How important are quality-of-life issues in examining the links between libraries and the economy? On the one hand, Shields points out, are librarians who fear the outcome of "efforts to transpose library services into production charts hanging behind a director's desk." But there are also a growing number who feel that the library must be able to measure its impact if it is to survive in the information age. Libraries must grapple with these questions as they enter into coalitions with other institutions. But, he stresses, "these coalitions are going to have to represent the consumers of library services as well as the practitioners of information access and delivery."

"Coalitions and Libraries" is the theme of Part Three. William Eshelman examines the topic in "Serving the Public Good: Coalitions for Free Library Services." In making a case for the involvement of libraries in coalitions, Eshelman declares that "libraries certainly can no longer 'go it alone.' " Although coalitions are essential for the "enlightened self interest" of libraries, they, in turn, have a great deal to offer other organizations engaged in mutual concerns. He warns us that building coalitions may be the only means of staving off threats to the public library system, particularly by officials in the Reagan administration who are "opposed to public services in general and libraries in particular."

In "The Effective Coalition," Joan C. Durrance analyzes the characteristics of a strong coalition. Durrance explains that coalitions form more frequently in the eighties for several reasons: "Sociologists have pointed out that the decline of mediating institutions in society 'has led to an erosion in the traditional source of consensus making.' During the past decade, traditional mediating institutions such as political parties have been superseded by special interest groups." In her view, coalitions are most effective when they "form quickly around an issue or topic precipitated by a governmental action or the activity of another actor in the public policy arena."

Robert Theobald's "Creating Coalitions for a New Social Agenda" warns us that we now face unprecedented social transformations which threaten the survival of our culture and of the human race. The traditional type of coalition, which has "typically fought for or against specific causes," is no longer adequate. Today's coalitions must attempt nothing less than changing our system of values: "Adopting these changes means making fundamental changes in American culture, transforming it from a culture of competition to one of cooperation." For libraries to assume their central position in meeting this challenge, he asserts they must be willing to reorganize the current library system in order to provide the kinds of information necessary to effect social change: "Many in the profession may shudder at making the changes required to meet today's challenges . . . but they cannot ignore them, and they must realize that failure to make choices is itself a process of change."

Patricia Glass Schuman, in her essay, "Libraries and Coalition Building," is fully confident in the ability of coalitions to exert their influence in society. In fact, she says, they "may be the only effective way we can change current societal directions so that all of us can achieve and live in a humane, just, democratic society." Nevertheless, Schuman says, their impact depends on how aggressively they pursue their goals. "On the whole, libraries do not yet appear to be strongly oriented towards actively reaching out to— and working effectively with—other organized groups or institutions working on broad public-interest questions."

"Ad Hoc Coalition Building: The Minnesota Experience," by Suzanne H. Mahmoodi and Roger D. Sween, reports on the efforts of library and information professionals in Minnesota to address the role of library and information services in economic development. Their report outlines a strategy for developing professional linkages with the state's economic community. Minnesota's efforts may be instructive to other ALA chapters and groups who wish to develop similar coalitions.

In "The Coalition on Government Information," Nancy Kranich reviews the American Library Association's strategy in organizing a coalition capable of focusing national attention on governmental efforts to limit public information and in developing broad support for improving access to government documents. She describes the steps involved in forming the coalition and in pursuing its goals. The coalition has been successful on several fronts, she notes, as evidenced by the pressure it brought to bear on the Senate to reject the nominee for the Archivist of the United States. "Without the vigilance and concern of organizations interested in preserving the public's right to know," Kranich warns, "access to government information could deteriorate."

What was the effect of the President's Program? Joseph A. Boissé and Carla J. Stoffle share the views of the participants in the Afterword. In spite of the wide variety of political and philosophical views represented by the audience, Boissé and Stoffle found that the group was united in their belief that libraries are vibrant institutions whose educative mission benefits society as a whole while ensuring and reaffirming one of the most fundamental democratic principles: free and equal access to information. Participants left with a greater sensitivity to the ideals reflected in the concept of the public good, and their individual and institutional contributions to it.

Libraries, Coalitions, and the Public Good has been published to show that libraries and librarians, working in concert with a broad spectrum of other organizations, can be an effective force for the public good. While fulfilling their public commitments, they must insure that the federal government fulfills its special responsibility to support libraries, not only because of their great importance to American education, to the American economy, and to the cultural life of this nation, but also because libraries ensure an informed citizenry.

Acknowledgments

The 1985 President's Program could not have been the great success that it was without the dedication of the President's Planning Committee. I would like to thank the following persons, who gave unstintingly of their time and effort. John N. Berry III, Louise Parker Berry, Joseph A. Boissé, Herbert Biblo, Gloria Coles, Miriam Crawford, Robert Croneberger, Arthur Curley, Marva L. DeLoach (who also compiled the index to this book), William R. Eshelman, Robert B. Ford, George Grant, Alice B. Ihrig, Sharad Karkhanis, Patricia Rom, Patricia Glass Schuman, Carla Stoffle, Patricia Tarin, Lucille Thomas, and Valerie P. Wilford. Special thanks go to the moderator for the day's program, former ALA president Eric Moon.

Others who provided assistance included Frank Dempsey and Amanda Rudd, the co-chairs for Local Arrangements, as well as my colleagues from Minnesota, Roger Sween, Joseph Kimbrough, and Suzanne Mahmoodi. Peggy Barber and the other ALA staff contributed enormously to the success of the program as well.

To Ken Fischer, who conducted the training session for discussion leaders and recorders at the conference, and to the 425 volunteers who came forward to participate, I express my warmest appreciation.

Finally, my thanks go to participating organizations, whose representatives were as active as ALA members in lending their support. Among these were: The National Education Association, American Association for Adult and Continuing Education, American Association of University Professors, American Federation of School Administrators, Association for Childhood Education International, Council for Liberal Learning, National Council of Teachers of English, American Association for the Advancement of Science, American Historical Association, American Society for Information Science, and a number of others.

From the publishing and library worlds were: The Special Libraries Association, American Association of Law Libraries, Council on Interracial Books for Children, American Booksellers Association, Association of American Publishers, Catholic Library Association, Independent Research Libraries Association, Medical Library Association, and many state library associations. Among the many other participating organizations were: The American Civil Liberties Union, National Association for the Advancement of Colored People, National Urban League, The Sierra Club, Citizens for a Better Environment, The American Federation of State, County, and Municipal Employees, Communications Workers of America, Illinois Professional Fire Fighters Association, Illinois Federation of Teachers, American Association of Retired Persons, American Planning Association, Better Business Bureau, League of Women Voters, National Recreation and Parks Association, American Management Association.

—E. J. Josey
School of Library and Information Science
University of Pittsburgh

Introduction: Forging Coalitions for the Public Good

E. J. Josey

Never before has there been a time for all members of our profession to come together in unity of purpose and spirit so that we can speak with one voice in support of quality library services for the American people. If we are to overcome zero funding for libraries in the federal budget, and if we are to obtain the proper recognition that should be given to libraries, it is more important than ever that librarians band together in a powerful unifying force to remind this nation that libraries not only support the demands of an information age but also ensure an informed citizenry, which is essential to a democratic republic.

We must not forget the words of Thomas Jefferson, who said:

> If a nation expects to be ignorant and free in a state of civilization, it expects what never was and never will be ... if we are to guard against ignorance and remain free, it is the responsibility of every American to be informed.

In the current period of stress and uncertainty for great numbers of the American people, it is desirable to reemphasize the unity of our goals with those of other leading organizations that are also concerned with the public interest, and to focus on building strong coalitions for the public good. While we continue to hone our own skills and improve the methods by which libraries provide information and recreational services, we need to develop

---

*Excerpted from E. J. Josey's American Library Association Presidential inaugural address, June 27, 1984.

new ways to explore the many common objectives that we share with other professionals and with community leaders.

Many will ask: "What do we mean by 'the public good'?" The phrase is well known and often used, but like other frequently used terms, its common acceptance may hide a failure to probe its meaning.

The term dates at least from Adam Smith's *Wealth of Nations,* but distortions of his theories permeate the contemporary business world and are influencing the outlook of many in library leadership. Smith supported the idea that public works are essential elements in the economy and that the State is obligated to provide financial support to those institutions that benefit the whole society and whose costs are so great that private individuals and organizations cannot provide such services.

Central to our efforts is the idea that the public good engenders general social benefits, rather than individual gain, pointing clearly to libraries as a first example of a public good that merits support from public funds. The "general welfare" phrase in the preamble to the U.S. Constitution epitomizes for most of us the purpose of activity in the public interest. The public good embraces the task of providing human services *without* sacrificing them to or putting them in competition with armaments, which leads to the well-known "guns or butter" debate.

The public good, in an even broader sense of the general welfare, is closely related to progress for libraries. In a time of attack on the basic freedoms and economic well-being of the most vulnerable sections of the population, professional groups must recognize their stake in the outcome of that attack and their responsibilities to support the freedoms and welfare of these people. Librarians therefore need to integrate their goals with the goals of greatest importance to the American people, e.g., the preservation of basic democratic liberties, the enlargement of equal opportunity for women and minorities, and the continuance of earlier national planning to raise the level of the educational and economic well-being of greater numbers of the population.

We need to foster and to reaffirm the inseparable relationship between libraries and democratic liberties. Our organizational problems may be more effectively resolved as we turn to the larger society and join with others in assisting the citizenry to use information services towards the solution of immediate social problems. There is, in fact, an obvious interconnection of public issues with library issues: the reduced availability and increasing cost of government sources of information limit the librarian's ability to provide information. Librarians are in a special position to know of restrictions on government information and to alert the public to act to force changes in policy when needed. The "right to know" and the "right to read" cannot be separated in the long run.

Economic self-interest is an obvious reason for joining with others to support the needs of the American people, and for combining that effort with public education on the value of libraries, both in an economic sense and in a broader social context. There is need to combat the recent government outlook that "information is not a free good" by emphasizing the substantial value of this information to those who cannot pay for it. One of our goals in this effort must be to stress the public sector's responsibility to support such institutions as the public library and its sister agencies, and to combat the present moves to consider information the property of the private sector. We need to put the public sector back where it was in the national consciousness as the responsible agent for institutions of public interest. This is a public responsibility of which individual taxpayers should be more aware. All sectors of government have the obligation to support libraries, but it is a part of our job as librarians to educate the public to respond to that obligation.

We must also clarify the direct effect of economics on the character of our services. Low budgets and fees for services can have the same result as censorship in limiting public access to ideas. But there is also the long-range negative effect of decisions made by librarians under economic pressure. When fees are charged for library services, the resulting assumption is that the services are not needed by the whole society and therefore do not deserve public support. And when "cost effectiveness" becomes our guide to which services will be offered—e.g., cutting branch libraries' hours without consulting the community, or eliminating outreach services when seed-money funding is lost— we further undermine potential tax support.

In adopting the theme of working for the public good through coalitions representing large segments of the American people, we are directly pursuing three of ALA's priorities: access to information, legislation and funding, and public awareness—and indirectly serving the cause of intellectual freedom.

PART ONE
Libraries and the Public Good

The Public Good:
What Is It?

John N. Berry III

Lighthouses. These save lives and cargos. But lighthouse keepers cannot reach out to collect fees from ships; nor would it serve an efficient social purpose for them to exact an economic penalty on ships who use their services. The light can be most efficiently provided free of charge, for it costs no more to warn 100 ships than to warn a single ship of the nearby rocks. We have here a positive externality, a divergence between private and social advantage. Philosophers and political leaders have always recognized the necessary role of government as provider of such goods.

So say economists Paul Samuelson and William D. Nordhaus, calling the lighthouse "a typical example of a public good provided by government service."[1]

My task is to define the term "public good," to define the broader concept of "the public good," to differentiate between the two (if possible), and, finally, to show why libraries, like lighthouses, are both public goods and nurture the public good.

GOVERNMENT SUPPORT OF THE PUBLIC GOOD

Among the philosophers and political leaders who have always recognized the necessary role of government is Adam Smith, whose writings spanned every discipline from astronomy to history, but whose contributions to what we now call the social sciences are best known. Smith, in his philosophical treatise the *Theory of Moral Sentiments*, gives us a good starting point. "Justice," he says, "is the main pillar that upholds the whole edifice. If it is removed, the great, the immense fabric of human society . . . must in a moment crumble into atoms."

Smith is popularly credited with giving us the fundamental principles of free enterprise or free market economics. He is surely the original source of the much-debated "supply side" theories, and although he died in 1790, many of his theories bear an uncanny resemblance to the views of the Reagan administration. Yet despite his belief in free trade unfettered by any interference from the state, from corporations, from monopoly, Smith still felt that government must play a role, particularly in a free society.

"Though the state," said Smith, "was to derive no advantage from the instruction of the inferior ranks of people, it would still deserve its attention to see that they should not be altogether uninstructed. He continued:

> The state derives no inconsiderable advantage from their instruction... They are more disposed to examine, and more capable of seeing through, the interested complaints of faction and sedition, and they are, upon that account, less apt to be misled into any wanton or unnecessary opposition to the measures of government. In free countries . . . the safety of government depends very much upon the favourable judgment which the people may form of its conduct [and] it must surely be of the highest importance that they should not be disposed to judge rashly or capriciously concerning it.

Smith defined two kinds of educational institutions: "those for the education of the youth, and those for the instruction of people of all ages." He defined education as a public good in the same way that today's economists define it: "The expense of the institutions for education . . . is . . . beneficial to the whole society, and may, therefore, without injustice, be defrayed by the general contribution of the whole society."

INFORMATION AS A PUBLIC GOOD

Samuelson and Nordhaus provide a modern definition of "public good":

> A commodity whose benefits may be provided to all people (in a nation or town) at no more cost than that required to provide it for one person. The benefits of the good are indivisible and people cannot be excluded. For example, a public health measure that eradicates smallpox protects all, not just those paying for vaccinations. To be contrasted with private goods, such as bread, which if consumed by one person, cannot be consumed by another person.

They cite other traditional examples of public goods: roads, national defense, the maintenance of internal law and order, the support of pure science, public health.

The economist Malcolm Getz, in his *Public Libraries: An Economic View*, adds knowledge and culture, saying they are "pure public goods, such that one individual's consumption need not subtract from the fund available for consumption by others, and indeed may even add to others' consumption."[2] Even Lawrence J. White, who asserts in his book *The Public Library in the 1980s* that the public library "does not meet the standard criteria of a public good," agrees that "information has the properties of a public good. Once it is in existence, one person can use it and benefit from it without using it up or interfering with the benefit enjoyed by other users." White also asserts that ". . . access clearly does have the properties of a public good. The extra costs for providing an additional person with access are very small or nonexistent." White brushes all the talk of access aside by saying:

> Most public library use by adults is not wholly or even primarily frivolous, but it would be hard to argue that most adult use of a public library brings anything close to the external benefits to society conveyed by children's and students' use. . . Ultimately, this question is related to the likelihood and value of use itself. Thus, we are led back to the other primary questions concerning the attributes of the library and its use; access by itself does not justify placing the public library into the category of public goods.[3]

In my view, that is arguable. Indeed, the notion of providing access to the accumulated information, knowledge, and wisdom of humankind is essential to our case. It is that function which the library performs best, and performs differently—better than any other institution for adult and child alike.

This idea is not new; I think it was Dan Lacy who first elaborated on the difference between access to information as found in a library and that found through other sources or media. My paraphrase goes like this: The broadcast media are forced to select from the immense information produced in modern times a small portion that will fit in a half-hour newscast or a daily paper. The information vendors aim their packages of information at carefully segmented markets that are chosen because they can afford the price; they need the very narrow and specific data, and thus return a profit to the vendor. They don't care as much about the number of people who buy access as they do about the return on their investment in making access available.

The library, on the other hand, collects all the knowledge of society, all the information, unedited, unscreened, unrewritten, and instead of broadcasting it to the masses, organizes and directs that information to the individual. The individual—Adam Smith would have liked that. Samuelson does.

So, although I disagree with Larry White's conclusions, his review of the criteria for designating a public good are useful to our analysis and our case. By charter, statute, and tradition, no one can be excluded from access to the information in a public library, from the use of that library, or from enjoying the benefits of that use.

LIBRARIES: A PUBLIC GOOD AT MINIMAL COST

The extra cost for the extra person to enjoy the benefits of that library, that public good, are very, very low. In fact, in absolute costs they are nearly zero. Public libraries, for their entire history, have never received more than two percent of the costs of municipal government in America. Two percent. Yet studies show that up to fifty percent of the population regularly use them. Even if fifty percent had always used the library, which we know is not true, that would mean that we are adding millions of users with every baby boom and still providing the service for a two percent pittance. No public good is so inexpensive. Look at defense, at highways, at postal service, at formal education.

To rebut White, then, in order to meet the criteria of Smith, Samuelson and Nordhaus, and Getz, and convince the economists that public libraries qualify as public goods, one has to buttress the notion that the fifty percent of the population currently using libraries on a regular basis does so for "serious" reasons, and that their use of the library has real benefits for society as a whole. While that case may seem self-evident to us, it is not necessarily so for those economists. Let's, at least, make the case, and discuss what elements are missing from its reality.

The case was best made by the trustees of the Boston Public Library as long ago as 1852, sixty-two years after Adam Smith died. In their wisdom they realized that they needed a public library, a public good. The private libraries that existed in Boston in 1852 didn't do the job: " . . . multitudes among us have no right of access to any one of the more considerable and important of these libraries," the trustees said, "and, except in rare cases, no library among [them] seeks to keep more than a single copy of any book on its shelves . . . no one of them, nor indeed, all of them taken together, can do even a tolerable amount of what ought to be done towards satisfying the demands for healthy nourishing reading made by the great masses of our people, who cannot be expected to purchase such reading for themselves." They added that the private circulating libraries of that time were also inadequate because they were, and I quote, "adventures and speculations for private profit."

Then they came to the point:

> . . . it has been rightly judged that—under political, social and religious institutions like ours—it is of paramount importance that the means of general information should be so diffused that the largest possible number of persons should be induced to read and understand questions going down to the very foundations of social order, which are constantly presenting themselves, and which we, as a people, are constantly required to decide, and do decide, either ignorantly or wisely. . . .

What about access?

> As to the terms on which access should be had to a City Library, the trustees can only say that they would place no restrictions on its use . . . regarding it as a great matter to carry as many books as possible into the home of the young, into poor families, into cheap boarding houses, in short, whenever they will be most likely to affect life and raise personal character and condition.

They called the library the "crowning glory of our system of city schools," and would make that library an institution "fitted," they said, "to continue and increase the best effects of that system."

Let's review the case: The library is cheap, costs about two percent, serves easily fifty percent. It provides those externalities the economists like so much: information for better living, better voting, better partaking of the culture.

It focuses on the individual, yet when that individual uses it properly, and it serves him or her properly, the whole society benefits in better informed decisions both in the marketplace and in the arenas of self-government. In that sense, not one single citizen can be excluded from its benefits—it clearly benefits all whenever any use it. Let me say that again: not one single citizen is excluded from individual use of that public good called the library, and whenever any citizen uses it the whole society benefits.

One thing we often overlook, and which is basic to arguments regarding public goods, is the fact that the library, by any measure, is efficient, and like the lighthouse, the library is more efficiently run by government and through taxation. Name any other source of information or recreation that serves half the people for that paltry two percent. Remember, public libraries, throughout their history and even now, never get more than two percent of the money spent on municipal government in America. Two percent! Name any private sector source of information that is that efficient. Name any public agency that does its job so well on so little. We often neglect that fact and feel guilty because more people don't use the library, but all studies show that library use ranges from thirty-five to fifty percent of the people. What other public service, what other public good, can claim that level of effi-ciency? So even there, at the bottom line, the public library serves more people, better, at lower costs, than any private or public sector manager can ever claim, and don't let any B-school economist, city manager, or politician tell you different.

That brings me to the point very quickly. All of this arcane theorizing by economists as to what qualifies as a public good is irrelevant. We really don't have to ask Adam Smith, or Larry White, or even our friend Paul Samuelson. Not in our country. Here in the U.S.A. we early on spelled out the functions of govern-ment . . . and we should really remind ourselves about that more often.

PUBLIC SUPPORT FOR LIBRARIES

Who governs America? The preamble to our basic law, our Constitution, is very clear about that. It begins with "We the people. . ." Why do we need that government? It spells out the reasons: "to form a more perfect Union. . . ." We need knowledge and information about ourselves for that task. We need learning and information to "establish justice. . . ." We need them to "insure domestic tranquility, to provide for the common defense. . . ." How can we promote the general welfare without education and full information? How can we "secure the blessings of liberty"? We must create a government to protect and deliver the learning and information that not only spells out what those blessings of to Information (the Lacy Commission) says, a key attribute of a public good is that no citizen can be excluded from its use. When we start worrying, as the Commission does, about the need to "prevent some users from abusing the libraries' resources . . ." or even when we hint, again as the Commission does, that our century-old policy of free library service must somehow be revised to accommodate some kind of fee for information in electronic formats, we violate that long-standing compact with the citizens.

Equally crucial, we admit that the services for which we charge are not public goods, and that it's O.K. to exclude certain classes of citizens from their use. Fees for library service automatically bring into question the status of libraries as public goods. Remember, if you can discriminate, if you can decide to end the benefits of library service to those who cannot pay, you no longer qualify as a public good. You are no longer worthy of tax support, and you may remember that somewhere between eighty and ninety-five percent of public library support comes from taxes.

Our job, our increasingly complex and difficult job as electronic formats and pressure to give our services and information over to a commodity model in a marketplace mounts, is to do the bidding of the citizens. From the beginning of our designation of libraries as a public good, those citizens have said that as a society we need, we must have, free public libraries. They are fundamental to democratic self-government.

The public knows what is a public good. The public knows what is the public good. And in our society, thank god, the public makes the decision.

Let us never oppose or violate that democratic trust. Let us never tell the public that better library service, more information, is only available to the privileged who can pay a fee. Let us never tell the public that you can only use the newest and best information sources, the electronic sources, if you are rich enough to afford the privilege. Let us, instead, form a coalition with that public to protect the public's right to that information in order to "secure the blessings of liberty" whether it is locked up in a vendor's online database, a publisher's book, a government's secret file, or a network's videotape.

Let us never tell the poor, or the old, or the young, or those who are out of power, that we can't afford to give them the information to "promote the general welfare."

Let us never tell those citizens who have supported us for so long that they are wrong, that libraries are not a public good, that liberty are but how we can protect them, nurture them, and record them for "ourselves and our posterity." The framers of the Constitution knew what a public good was, and what the publi good was.

As it turns out, Americans have never been at a loss to defin them ever since. No, it isn't a perfect Union yet. But for mor than two centuries, we have agreed on a few elements of that goo government, and one of those elements has been the public library We don't have to ask the economists, and the academics, and th managers and politicians, because we the people have supporte libraries from their beginnings. We've supported them in goo times and bad based on our knowledge as citizens that, to gover ourselves, we must be informed. The citizens, the voters, hav supported the library ever since, in good times and bad.

Who was it, almost immediately after the public had voted fc the infamous Proposition 13 in California, that restored lost ta revenues and more to the Berkeley Public Library? The voter And in that same state, very soon after Proposition 13, a pc showed that while they opposed an unfair tax system, those Ca fornia voters would, by a margin of two to one, pay higher taxes the money would go to education. Who was it who marched c the chambers of the city council in Newark some fifteen years ag when that body had voted to close the Newark Public Library? was the citizens, most of whom, incidentally, used the institutic infrequently. They said, in thousands of voices and hundreds ways, "No, you can't take our library." They admitted, "No, v don't use it every day, even every month, but it protects us whe we need it. It keeps the record straight; it keeps the informatic we need available." And they won.

Ask Jane Morgan who finally came to the rescue of the Detrc Public Library after years of abuse at the hands of city, state, ar federal government. Once again, it was the voters. And again the said, "No, you can't take away our library." Ask Keith Doms ho easy it is to close a library branch in Philadelphia; or Varta Gregorian in New York; or Marilyn Mason in Atlanta; or Bern Margolis up in Monroe County, Michigan; or Ginnie Cooper Alameda County; or Jack Franz in San Francisco; or Bill Sannwa in San Diego; or Pat Woodrum in Tulsa; or Agnes Griffin in Mor gomery County.

It is that citizen support that is crucial to the future libraries and to their status as public goods. Remember, despi what that ALA Commission on Freedom and Equality of Acce they are unworthy of that support. Let us never tell them that they offer two kinds of service—you know how that goes—"basic" service for everyone, and the other service, the new stuff that's reserved for the privileged, the privileged who can pay, who are certified to be sound security risks, who hold office or power.

Let us never turn away a citizen because he or she is too young, too old, or his or her inquiry is "frivolous" or somehow, as the Lacy report puts it, "abuses" the right of access to a library.

Let us never be frightened away because that mission, defending what the public has defined as a public good, seems so immense, so difficult. Let us not be discouraged because from time to time the society turns away from government, or rebels against an unfair tax system. In those times of darkness, politicians will try to lock up the records of how they govern. Slick entrepreneurs will try to convince us to pay again for their reprint of the government information we've already paid for because they somehow give "added value" to that free good. Marketers will try to force every fact, everything we need to know, into the ubiquitous marketplace, that marketplace which is inaccessible to those who are out of work, out of money, and out of hope.

When darkness falls, as it does from time to time in the affairs of humanity, let us brighten the beacon from our lighthouses, let us show the way to avoid the rocks, reefs, and hidden gates of privilege that block the ship of state as it heads for that harbor of democratic self-government. As Samuelson pointed out, those lighthouses, those classic public goods, save lives and cargo. The intellectual and information lighthouse that is the library saves democracy. It must never be darkened.

REFERENCES

1. Paul Samuelson and William D. Nordhaus, *Economics*, 12th ed. (New York: McGraw-Hill, 1985).
2. Malcolm Getz, *Public Libraries: An Economic View* (Baltimore: Johns Hopkins University Press, 1980), p. 24.
3. Lawrence White, *The Public Library in the 1980s* (Lexington, Mass: Lexington Books, 1983), pp. 126–137.

The Library's Commitment to the Public Sector

Fay M. Blake

Mohandas Gandhi once said: "My notion of democracy is that under it the weakest should have the same opportunity as the strongest." It's a notion that has on some occasions swept American society, but a notion that, unfortunately, America in the 1980s disregards. We have been willing to define the public good merely as that which is good for some at the expense of others and that which can best be obtained by private effort without concern for those individuals who have not succeeded—the poor, the homeless, the hungry, and the disregarded. Arthur Miller, speaking at a colloquium at the University of East Anglia in July 1984, characterized our age as one in which "we're living in the wash of great ideals that have risen and fallen into the sea." One of those great ideals is the belief that the public good is neither public nor good as long as anyone is denied access to a life worth living.

Today many of us seem to be busy denying the existence of the poor among us while evidence accumulates that poverty in the United States is steadily increasing. Non-partisan governmental reports have revealed that half a million people are living below the poverty level as a direct result of cuts in social programs since 1982, that more than 325,000 families lost eligibility for Aid to Families with Dependent Children during this period, and that at least seventeen million families have annual incomes of less than $7000.

Poverty in the United States not only persists, but grows. The latest Census Bureau Report (August 2, 1984) stated that from 1982 to 1983, the number of poor people grew to 35.3 million, an increase of 868,000. The average income of the poorest one-fifth

16

of all families declined by eight percent, from $6913 to $6391, reported a major study of the Urban Institute, released August 15, 1984. New York City's economy is ebullient, say its restaurant, movie house, and hotel owners, but the Federal Bureau of Labor Statistics announced that almost a million New Yorkers are on welfare; that every fourth New Yorker is below the federal poverty level; and that more people at any time since the Depression are homeless and hungry. The Reagan administration reported gleefully in 1984 that the national unemployment rate was "only" 7.5 percent, but the Joint Economic Committee of the Congress glumly added two and a half million unemployed people to the reported 8.5 million, "the phantom unemployed" who have dropped out of the labor force, bringing the national unemployment figures to 9.7 percent. And the national figure hides the reality of appalling unemployment rates among certain groups in our society: over forty percent among black males and over sixty percent among black teenagers. Women still receive only a little over half the salary of white males and are increasingly the sole supporters of their children; blacks, browns, Asians, and Native Americans are still crowded into lower paid jobs or are out of work entirely; the disabled are still denied access to jobs and constitute many of the poor.

What is evident from this array of statistics is that some people in our country are suffering, but what may not be so evident is that these people constitute a minority of our total population, and a politically powerless minority at that. What is even less evident from the figures themselves is our national willingness to write these people off precisely because they are a powerless minority. We have become receptive to the mostly tacit but strong assumption that all's well because most of us are surviving fairly well.

So far, the statistics have been confined to the United States. If we were to begin to contemplate the global picture, we might find it a bit more difficult, although a lot more tempting, to turn away and devote ourselves to our usual daily problems: paying the bills, earning a living, taking a vacation, attending a conference. Nobel Prize Winner Gabriel Garcia Marquez, in his acceptance speech in Stockholm, talked not about literature but about the twenty million starving children in South America. Another renowned writer, Gunter Grass, commented: "To be sure, we can make great new discoveries with our technological skill and scientific ability—we can split the atom, see to the end of the universe, and reach the moon. But these milestones of human progress occur in the midst of a society sunk in a statistically proven barbarism. All those atom splitters, those conquerors of space, those who punctually feed their computers and gather, store and evaluate all their data; none is in a position to provide sufficient food for the children of this world."

Confronted by the global magnitude of poverty—fifteen million children dead of disease and malnutrition in 1984, ten million children under sixteen in Brazil abandoned on the streets— we can only turn away, look for brighter reports, try to blunt our sense of outrage and helplessness. As another Nobel Prize Winner, Heinrich Boll, put it: "Everything is geared towards driving us to distraction and stupefaction. Everything is smiled away, laughed off in the vacuousness of conferences, the emptiness of summits and the hollowness of that done-to-death word, 'solidarity.'"

Well, what should we do about the problems of poverty? What can we do? We need, first of all, to recognize the extent of the problem. We need to have a sense of outrage, unfashionable as moral indignation is these days. And we need to turn right-side-up the callous, nonsensical economic, political, and social "wisdom" which defines the public good as what's good for the majority. If that's a heresy, let's make the most of it. The public good is the welfare and quality of life of *all* of us throughout the globe, and the constituency of the public sector is precisely that portion of the population which has not made it—the poor and the disregarded. Historian Henry Steele Commager, in a recent letter to *The New York Times*, reminded us all that the disappearance of political leadership in American life is not only lamentable but reversible. "The solution to the current drought," he maintains, "might not be in more formal training (whether in leadership, in wisdom or in virtue) but in a shift in the center of gravity in American life and thought from private to public enterprise and from commitment to individual wealth to the commonwealth."

In the face of shrinking public funds and resources, and even more cogently, in the face of a philosophical retreat from collective public solutions, many elements of the public sector have sought some sort of help or relationship with private industry. At the lowest level, this takes the ignominious form of going hat in hand to beg for a handout. Is the local public television channel about to fold? Ask Bechtel or Mobil for a sizeable contribution. Are public job and training programs crippled? Ask Levi Strauss or Bank of America to help out. But more and more public entities are turning to private business for help in much more involved ways. Atlantic City, for example, is calling on the gambling casinos for help in rebuilding the city. And New Brunswick, New Jersey, has made the giant pharmaceutical company Johnson and Johnson a partner in the revitalization of the city. An examination of these partnerships reveals, however, that the benefits are less than equitably distributed and that the poor are not the beneficiaries. In Atlantic City, for example, the mayor called for a $246 million housing and commercial redevelopment. In a city plagued by high unemployment, people need low-income subsidized housing. H. Steven Norton, executive vice president of Resorts International, disagrees: "Atlantic City should not be building more subsidized housing....What...[it] needs for revitalization is an influx of more affluent residents." What the casino executives want is "to be allowed to put some of their reinvestment money into municipal projects that would directly benefit them, such as widening roadways and improving water and sewage services in their part of town."

In New Brunswick, a development corporation headed by Johnson and Johnson's chairman and a planning corporation headed by its corporate vice president for administration used private funds to buy land, lease it to developers, and encourage them by means of city tax concessions and zoning changes. What Johnson and Johnson has wrought is a downtown New Brunswick gleaming with Johnson and Johnson corporate headquarters, a Hyatt Hotel partly owned by Johnson and Johnson, and luxurious office buildings expensive new shopping malls and gourmet restaurants. But H. Briavel Holcomb, chair of the urban planning department at nearby Rutgers University, noted that "the city's shortage of housing remains critical."

Edward Bloustein, president of Rutgers, admitted "the plan is driving people out of center city and giving them the short end of the redevelopment stick." He added, however, "Nevertheless, there is a marked degree of success. There are tangible signs of people enjoying the city they couldn't enjoy before." Professor Holcomb countered: "The new and planned construction has enhanced the city's image, but in a fashion that serves primarily Johnson and Johnson and its desire to have its world headquarters placed in an appropriate physical setting." Once again, the poor are the disregarded, and for the sake of jobs for some, an "enhanced image," and some sparkling new luxury toys, we have been willing to forget the commitment of the public sector to the public good.

Even with such a philosophical commitment, however, we shall never be able to make a difference to the poor without a basic turn in our national and global priorities. Poverty in this country and in the world cannot be eradicated or alleviated as long as ever-scarcer resources are expended on wasteful and destructive engines of war. It must be our first priority in our concern for the public good to learn for ourselves and to teach others that, in the words of Congressman Ronald Dellums of California: "The perpetuation of the permanent war economy is truly looting the means of production in our society and costing this nation literally millions of productive jobs every year." We need to remember Martin Luther King's challenge: "We have flown the air like birds and swum the sea like fishes, but we have not learned the simple act of walking the earth like brothers."

For librarians to dedicate themselves to the poor as a means of redefining the public good may make our work more difficult. It involves finding out the information needs of a minority whom we, along with most other professionals, have overlooked. We must discover how they can learn skills, obtain food, find housing, demand legislation, and change budget priorities. We must find ways to present that information in usable form. To perform this almost unprecedented task, we can learn from the wisdom of Paulo Freire, one of the world's greatest teachers of illiterates:

> Those who authentically commit themselves to the people must re-examine themselves constantly. This conversion is so radical as not to allow of ambiguous behavior. To affirm this commitment but to consider oneself the proprietor of revolutionary wisdom—which must then be given to (or imposed upon) the people—is to retain the old ways. The man who proclaims devotion to the cause of liberation yet is unable to enter into communion with the people, whom he continues to regard as totally ignorant, is grievously self-deceived.

In other words we must learn from this minority, from the dispossessed and "ignorant," how to provide them with the information they need to change a society which has deprived them of a full life. Therein lies the most potent coalition we can create—a coalition of equals in which our skills are put at the disposal of those who need them. The development of such a coalition is one of the hardest of all tasks facing librarians in the public sector. A real commitment to an untraditional public may mean a lessening of personal service to our traditional middle class users. We may have to let them find their own way to the information they need.

But many in our traditional public have the education and money to seek and find alternative information sources. And many have the self-confidence to demand the attention of the public sector.

It's the dispossessed, often lacking the means to find what they can use, whom we must help by reeducating ourselves, our communities, our friends; by developing programs for people who "never come near the library"; and by seeking their knowledge and advice. This may open a new and exciting professional life for us. Sue Hubbell, who has been writing a series of enchanting accounts in *The New York Times* of her life as a beekeeper, described herself as "a wimpish librarian at Brown University" before she found fulfillment in another vocation. A new commitment to the public good may renew a sense of fulfillment for librarians within their own profession. And it may help to move our society from a destructive to a life-giving course.

The Public Good: The Independent Sector's Point of View

Virginia Ann Hodgkinson

Not since the time of the Depression has there been so much public discussion about the roles and responsibilities of government, the marketplace, and the independent sector (also called the voluntary, nonprofit, philanthropic, or third sector). Each of these sectors performs various functions in our society—and each in its own way serves the public good. But in the past half century, the roles and the responsibilities among these sectors have not been so questioned—nor in many ways so confused—as they have been since 1980. Resolving the debate on the relative roles of these three sectors of American society in serving the public good—particularly the roles of government and the independent sectors—is of immense importance to all of us.

Perhaps from the outset, I ought to say that the private sector cannot serve the public good without relationships with government and the for-profit sectors of our society. These relationships have existed in one form or another since colonial times. The question is not so much how each sector differs, but rather, what is the relative balance among the roles and responsibilities among these sectors? What are the responsibilities as well as the limitations of each of these sectors in serving the public good? What public goods ought to be accomplished within our highly complex, diverse, and pluralistic society by government, by the independent sector, or by the for-profit sector? The questions we have been asking as a society are: Which sector does what? For whom? Who pays? Who benefits? The answers to these questions are not easy, for many of the answers are premised on the acceptance of a set of common values that Americans can agree on. That's one of the basic functions of the independent sector—to provide a forum for developing consensus about public issues that are of importance to a majority of Americans.

THE INDEPENDENT SECTOR

The independent sector in the American experience preceded formal government. Daniel J. Boorstin has commented that citizens in America could choose their communities rather than being born into them. He suggests that this element of choice increased citizen involvement and responsibility to community. In nineteenth century Europe, governments already held primary responsibility for many activities of society, but the "decisive fact, not sufficiently noticed, is that in America, even in modern times, *communities* existed before governments were here to care for public needs. There were many groups of people with a common sense of purpose and a feeling of duty to one another before there were political institutions forcing them to perform their duties."[1] This capacity of Americans to band together to engage in activities to serve the public good is the essence of the independent sector and, perhaps, one of the most distinctive features of American society.

Most Americans have heard the most quoted phrase from de Tocqueville[2] that Americans constantly formed associations of all kinds to serve religious, moral, recreational, civic, professional, and other serious and social purposes. This habit of forming associations has lasted throughout our history. In fact, another distinguished American historian, Merle Curti, has suggested that the habit of citizens to voluntarily join together to engage in activities for the public good has become a distinctive part of the American character.[3] These character traits of giving and volunteering were shaped in part by our colonial experience, and later through the selection of federalism as our form of government.

Perhaps even more profoundly, this habit of citizen community action was shaped by the nature of our government, with its built-in checks and balances, its separation of church and state, and its constitutional protection of individual freedom. The constitutional separation of powers among the branches of the federal government and the decentralization of power to the states and citizens has led to strong citizen involvement and responsibilities in local, state, and national issues.

Most of the great social institutions and social movements of our society were started in the independent sector. For example, we talk about public libraries as a social good. Most Americans would agree that libraries should receive continuing support from local taxpayers and, to a lesser degree, the federal government. But this support of the concept of free public libraries grew out of the establishment of a subscription library founded by Benjamin Franklin. It was not until Andrew Carnegie decided to donate a substantial part of his fortune to the support of this public good that the public library movement took hold. Carnegie donated a total of $56.1 million from his fortune to establish 2,501 libraries in the U.S., Canada, and other countries. He believed that the "best gift" that could be given to a community was a free library "provided that the community will accept and maintain it as a public institution, as much a part of the city property as its public schools, and, indeed, as an adjunct to these."[4]

At the turn of the century, as our nation became urbanized, it became necessary to increase the government's responsibility for the poor, for social welfare, for health, for social insurance, and for research in order to provide an equitable distribution of services to citizens as well as to carrying on the nation's business, much of which is now handled through a multiplicity of government, nonprofit, and for-profit institutions and organizations.

Whereas we do know a lot about government and for-profit enterprise, we know very little about this third or independent sector of American life. Waldemar Nielsen, author of *The Endangered Sector*, speaks eloquently on our lack of knowledge about this "peculiar" sector:

> Its peculiarity lies in the fact that although the institutions that embody it are all around us and constitute an important part of our lives, we remain largely unaware of it. The simple statistics about it are not collected; scholars rarely study it; our teachers don't teach about it. It represents a huge sector of our American pluralistic system—operating in parallel to the sectors of government and the business economy—yet there is not even an accepted name for it.[5]

THE STRUCTURE OF THE SECTOR

The independent sector is very diverse. It contains both the great institutions of our society as well as countless thousands of associations serving a diverse number of purposes.

Its institutions include our nation's churches, synagogues and mosques; thousands of private hospitals; colleges, universities, and schools; museums, libraries, and symphony orchestras; free-standing research institutions and private foundations.

Its associations cover a whole range of public interests; youth development; civil rights; the protection of animals; civic activities; professional organizations; the prevention of diseases; the preservation of historical buildings; the support of music, art, and libraries; and public and private education, to name but a few. Thus, the American Library Association, the oldest library association supporting librarianship and the spread of libraries, is very much a part of this long American tradition.

Recent estimates of the size and diversity of the independent sector are impressive. It includes an estimated 785,000 organizations, including over 325,000 churches. Its estimated revenues in 1980 were $212 billion, including $52 billion from contributed volunteer time; $44.7 billion in contributions; $61.7 billion in dues, fees and charges; $40.3 billion from government; and $13.2 billion from other sources of income. Its estimated employment was 10.2 million people in 1980—6.2 million were paid employees and over 80 million adults contributed time equivalent to that of 4.1 million full-time employees, comprising over forty percent of its total employment.[6]

THE FUNCTIONS OF THE INDEPENDENT SECTOR

More than a decade ago in November 1973, the Commission on Private Philanthropy and Public Needs was established as a privately funded effort to accomplish two major objectives: "to study the role of both philanthropic giving in the United States and that area through which giving is principally channeled, the voluntary, 'third' sector of American society," and "to make recommendations to the voluntary sector, to Congress and to the American public at large concerning ways in which the sector and the practice of private giving can be strengthened and made more effective." The commission worked for two years and produced its final report with recommendations: *Giving in America.*[7] In this report, the commission enumerated the various functions of voluntary groups and associations:

1. *"Initiating new ideas and processes"*: The independent sector is adept at innovating and experimenting with new ideas and

providing new models that may be used by government. Non-profit groups have experimented with innovations in health maintenance and birth control, and in new directions in research and analysis. Once their worthiness has been demonstrated, such innovations can be supported and expanded by government. "Nongovernmental organizations, precisely because they are nongovernmental and need to be attuned to a broad and diverse constituency, can take chances, experiment in areas where legislators and government agencies are hesitant to tread."

2. *"Developing public policies"*: Nonprofit organizations can influence and support government policy by engaging in research and public discussion in areas where government is involved or may get involved. Organizations at the local, regional, and national levels—such as the Brookings Institution, the Urban Institute, and the American Enterprise Institute—are constantly engaged in research in a variety of issues of national concern, such as health, social security, or the federal budget process. These groups can focus on long-term policy issues to help clarify and define them and to put them forth for public discussion in ways that government cannot easily do.

3. *"Supporting minority or local interests"*: Voluntary associations can support nonmajoritarian interests of society and set the agenda for these interests that previously went unrecognized by government. Thus the civil rights movement grew out of the work of the NAACP and other nonprofit groups, as did the women's, consumers', and environmental movements. Nonprofit groups can serve interests that tend to be local or too small for government, such as social service programs for smaller religious and ethnic groups, for refugees, or for migrant workers. Because of their capacity to function at the local level, these services can be delivered more humanely and efficiently. Essentially, such organizations preserve the rights and freedoms of all citizens even though they may be in a minority population.

4. *"Providing services that the government is constitutionally barred from providing"*: Under the U.S. Constitution, government cannot enter the broad category of religion. Religious functions must be carried out by the nonprofit sector. Other

functions, such as oversight of the news media, are better dealt with by nonprofit organizations rather than government because such government oversight could be regarded as an infringement of freedom of speech.

5. *"Overseeing government"*: Even with all the checks and balances provided in our type of government, government cannot be expected to police itself. Nonprofit organizations can monitor government—its action or its inaction and possibly even its excesses. In fact, the Commission on Private Philanthropy and Public Needs stated that as "government's role in many areas formerly dominated by nongovernmental groups grows ever larger, and the voluntary role grows correspondingly smaller, the monitoring and influencing of government may be emerging as one of the single most important and effective functions of the private nonprofit sector."

6. *"Overseeing the marketplace"*: Nonprofit organizations can oversee the marketplace without the economic interests of government and for-profit enterprise. Such organizations have been active in consumer movements, product safety, and environmentalism. Nonprofit institutions, such as hospitals or schools, working in competition with government and private enterprise provide alternatives and help to maintain the quality and innovation in all these institutions.

7. *"Bringing the sectors together"*: Nonprofit organizations help to bring together both government and business to serve public purposes. This is particularly true in community development organizations where these groups can bring together officials from business and government to collaborate in the interest of the public good.

8. *"Giving aid abroad"*: For many decades, workers from American nonprofit groups have been able to provide aid and technical services overseas, particularly in areas where there is sensitivity to U.S. government policies. Organizations like CARE, the Red Cross, and the American Friends Committee have been able to help victims of disasters overseas and to engage in technical assistance and economic development projects.

9. *"Furthering active citizenship and altruism"*: Voluntary groups serve as outlets for citizens to engage in public activities. With the restrictions upon government and its bureaucratic work arrangements, citizens can find the means to engage in activities to serve the public interest through these associations. Waldemar Nielsen finds this activity one of the main ways that citizens find an outlet for their altruism. "One of the most distinctive and commendable features of our society, voluntarism embodies a profoundly important concept—namely that a good citizen of a decent society has a personal responsibility to serve the needs of others."[8] The Commission concluded that altruism and active citizen involvement are "of the very essence in a healthy democratic society."

One of the major recommendations that came out of the Commission on Private Philanthropy and Public Needs was to develop an organization of national stature to gather information about the independent sector and its activities, to inform the public about this sector, to act as a liaison between this sector and government, and to preserve and strengthen this sector and its contributions to American life. Although a quasi-governmental organization was not formed, a new private organization, Independent Sector was founded in 1980 to perform some of these functions.

Four years after its founding, membership in Independent Sector has grown to nearly six hundred national voluntary organizations, foundations, and corporations. A sample of a few of its members reveals the scope and diversity of its membership: Accountants for the Public Interest, American Association for the Advancement of Science, American Association of Homes for the Aging, the American Association for Higher Education, the American Association of Museums, American Bar Association, the American Cancer Society, American Farmland Trust, Fluor Corporation, the Ford Foundation, the Monsanto Company, the NAACP Legal Defense and Education Fund, the National Alliance for the Mentally Ill, the National Association of Independent Colleges and Universities, the National Audubon Society, the National Catholic Conference, Inc., the National Council of LaRaza, the National Trust for Historic Preservation, the Russell Sage Foundation, the Rockefeller Foundation, the Schering-Plough Corporation, Second Harvest.

Working on common goals, the organizations involved in Independent Sector—a "network of networks"[9] as its current

Chairman of the Board, Richard Lyman, President of the Rocke-feller Foundation, has described it—have made measurable progress toward preserving and strengthening giving, volunteering, and not-for-profit activity in America. To mention but a few: helping to pass legislation for a charitable contributions deduction for tax-payers who do not itemize; producing the film "To Care: America's Voluntary Spirit"; publishing a book of readings on the sector, *America's Voluntary Spirit*, edited by Brian O'Connell; commissioning various national surveys on giving and volunteering; publishing the first statistical profile of the sector, *Dimensions of the Independent Sector*; working with coalitions to maintain reasonable postal rates for nonprofit institutions; and providing the secretariat and leadership for a coalition which has successfully opposed revisions in the Management and Budget Circular A-122, which would have seriously curtailed advocacy activities of non-profit groups. It's still a young organization, but it has demon-strated to itself and others that this "network of networks" can collaborate and work together to strengthen this sector.

THE EFFECTS OF FEDERAL BUDGET
CUTBACKS ON NONPROFIT ORGANIZATIONS
AND THE PEOPLE THEY SERVE

Since 1980, the Reagan administration has recommended several budget cutbacks in federal social programs and advised that the private and not-for-profit sectors take more responsibility for these programs. The respective roles and responsibilities of govern-ment, the not-for-profit, and the for-profit sectors are now at the center of a national debate. Fortunately for all of us, there are many nonprofit organizations studying the impact of the federal budget cuts and engaging in public discussion about the respon-sibilities of these sectors.

The Urban Institute, under the direction of Lester Salamon, has been conducting a study of the impact of federal budget cuts on nonprofit institutions. He recently reported the findings of his first survey. From 1980 to 1984, in constant 1980 dollars, federal funding other than for medicaid and medicare has dropped twenty-seven percent for all other sectors of nonprofit activity. The decline for social services was thirty-five percent; for civic and social organizations, twenty-two percent; for education and re-search, sixteen percent; for foreign aid, twenty-five percent; and for arts and culture, fifty percent. The total federal cutbacks in these areas from 1980 in 1980 constant dollars is over $29 billion.[10]

Salamon reported that some nonprofits were hurt more than others, and that private charity could not make up for federal budget cuts, even though private philanthropy has increased. Some agencies, such as arts and cultural organizations, made up revenues by increasing fees for services. He reported that even though the charitable sector held its own in 1981 and 1982, "it was not in a position to expand its services to fill in for the much larger reduction of direct government services in these fields." In fact, he concludes that although the administration supported increased voluntarism as a viable alternative for the delivery of services, "by pursuing a serious assault on a broad range of domestic programs that help to sustain the sector financially, without accompanying this with a positive program of action, the administration may have set back its own private-sector agenda for sometime to come and discredited voluntarism further as a serious policy alternative."[11]

Not only were there federal budget cuts in nonprofit organizations, but in all the areas where governmental, nonprofit, and for-profit organizations are active in the delivery of services through federal social programs. Overall, other than medicare and medicaid, federal expenditures from 1980 to 1984 in 1980 constant dollars declined fifteen percent, or approximately $15 billion dollars from $99.2 to $84.2 billion in these areas. Percentage declines in federal funding from 1980 to 1984 for all of social welfare was thirty-five percent; for education and research (including libraries), twenty-two percent; in health services, twenty-three percent; in arts and culture, seventeen percent; and for the environment, forty-three percent. There were slight overall increases for funding in income assistance and international aid. Medicare and medicaid expenses increased by twenty-two percent over this period.[12]

In another study conducted by the American Enterprise Institute titled *Meeting Human Needs*, which looked at new and more efficient ways for delivering services to citizens, editor Jack Meyer concluded that although more efficient and cost-effective delivery mechanisms could be developed for servicing human needs, "meeting these basic human needs for the disadvantaged is a responsibility of government. These problems are national in scope and will not be resolved by devolving them to lower levels of government. Such a step would foster an uneven access to basic social services across geographic boundaries."[13]

The discussion of the relative roles and responsibilities among the sectors continues. Many of the studies are supported by various research institutions within the independent sector. Representatives from government, industry, and the independent sector are working together to try to understand these roles through study groups, citizens' commissions, and research institutions. Again, this sector provides a forum where such discussion can go on unobstructed by the economic or political interests of government or private industry.

FORGING COALITIONS FOR THE PUBLIC GOOD

The theme of forging coalitions for the public good is very much a part of the basic purposes and functions of the independent sector. In fact, we truly are concerned about the necessity for more coalitions to serve the public good. John Gardner has written about the need for more *unum* and less *pluribus* in the hope that many organizations—as they strive to support their public interests— also remember "our shared concerns as a nation."[14]

Our pluralistic philosophy invites each organization, institution, or special group to develop its own potentialities. But the price of that treasured autonomy and self-preoccupation is that each institution also concern itself with the common good. That is not idealism; it is self-preservation. If the larger system fails, the subsystems fail. If the nation fails we all fail.[15]

Richard Lyman, in "What Kind of Society Shall We Have," asserts that "the promotion of the public good is our justification for being" in the independent sector. "We must see diversity not as an end in itself, but a powerful means to an end, the strengthening of the total society, and the enhancement of opportunities for all of its members. Whatever the sub-publics to which we owe allegiance, let us be quick to recognize the interests of others, and eager to identify the common interest that binds us all."[16]

The Independent Sector encourages such public discussions and the building of coalitions within the sector to serve the common good. As a "network of networks" itself, it is a coalition of organizations working toward preserving giving, volunteering, and not-for-profit initiative. It believes that this part of American life, in itself, fosters democratic values and maintains our individual freedom. We believe that the independent sector of American society represents a public good.

REFERENCES

1. Daniel Boorstin, "From Charity to Philanthropy" in Brian O'Connell, editor, *America's Voluntary Spirit A Book of Readings* (New York: The Foundation Center). pp. 129-131.
2. Alexis de Tocqueville, "Of the Use Which the Americans Make of Public Associations in Civil Life," *op. cit.* pp. 53-54.
3. Merle Curti, "American Philanthropy and the National Character," *op. cit.* pp. 161-179.
4. Margaret Beckman, Stephen Langmead, John Black, *The Best Gift: A Record of the Carnegie Libraries in Ontario* (Toronto: Dundurn Press, 1984). pp. 17-18.
5. Waldemar A. Nielsen, "The Third Sector: Keystone of a Caring Society" (Washington, D.C.: Independent Sector, 1980). p. 2.
6. Hodgkinson, Virginia A. and Weitzman, Murray, *Dimensions of the Independent Sector: A Statistical Profile* (Washington, D.C.: Independent Sector, 1984). pp. 1-18.
7. *Giving in America: Toward a Stronger Voluntary Sector*, Report of the Commission on Private Philanthropy and Public Needs (Washington, D.C.: Commission on Private Philanthropy and Public Needs, 1975). p. 1.
8. Nielsen, "The Third Sector . . . ," *op. cit.* pp. 41-46.
9. Richard W. Lyman, "What Kind of Society Shall We Have?" (Washington, D.C.: Independent Sector, 1981). p. 7.
10. Lester M. Salamon, "Nonprofit Organizations: The Lost Opportunity" in John L. Palmer and Isabel V. Sawhill, editors, *The Reagan Record* (Cambridge, Mass.: Ballinger Publishing Company). p. 278.
11. Ibid., pp. 284-285.
12. Ibid., p. 277.
13. Jack A. Meyer, editor, *Meeting Human Needs: Toward a New Public Philosophy* (Washington, D.C.: American Enterprise Institute for Public Policy Research, 1982). p. 29.
14. John W. Gardner, *Excellence*, Revised Edition (New York: W.W. Norton & Company, 1984). p. 139.
15. Ibid., pp. 139-140.
16. Lyman, *loc. cit.*

BIBLIOGRAPHY

Beckman, Margaret, Stephen Langmead and John Black. *The Best Gift: A Record of the Carnegie Libraries in Ontario* (Toronto: Dundurn Press, 1984).

Gardner, John W., *Excellence*. Revised edition (New York: W. W. Norton & Company, 1984).

Giving in America: Toward a Stronger Voluntary Sector. Report of the Commission on Private Philanthropy and Public Needs Washington, D.C.: Commission on Private Philanthropy and Public Needs, 1975.

Hodgkinson, Virginia A. and Murray Weitzman, *Dimensions of the Independent Sector: A Statistical Profile* (Washington, D.C. 1984).

Lyman, Richard W., "What Kind of Society Shall We Have?" Washington, D.C.: Independent Sector, 1981.

Meyer, Jack A., ed., *Meeting Human Needs: Toward a New Public Philosophy* (Washington, D.C.: American Enterprise Institute for Public Policy Research, 1982).

Nielsen, Waldemar A., "The Third Sector: Keystone of a Caring Society." Washington, D.C.: Independent Sector, 1980.

O'Connell, Brian, ed., *America's Voluntary Spirit: A Book of Readings* (New York: The Foundation Center, 1983).

Palmer, John L. and Isabel V. Sawhill, eds., *The Reagan Record* (Cambridge, Mass.: Ballinger Publishing Company, 1984).

Weicher, John J., ed., *Maintaining the Safety Net: Income Redistribution Programs in the Reagan Administration* (Washington, D.C.: American Enterprise Institute for Public Policy Research, 1984).

Towards a Broader Definition of the Public Good

Arthur Curley

It's been said many times that the greatest resource of the American Library Association is its membership. We come to conferences and battle over how many dollars will go into this aspect of the ALA budget and how many will go into that. But the time, energy, resources, talents, and ideas of the many thousands of ALA members are, I believe, truly our greatest resource. The kind of challenge inherent in the theme of forging coalitions for the public good is one that can't be left to a small and overworked staff at ALA headquarters or to a small number of people on the key committees of the association. It's something that really does require a massive commitment on the part of the full membership.

Public libraries and the public good: It's very interesting that the economist Adam Smith is the man generally credited with coining the phrase "public good" in that his conservative philosophy, ruthless by some standards, has had a very significant influence on the development of opinions less than sympathetic to the public good. Yet even Adam Smith acknowledged that there is a major component of public need which can not be addressed through the operation of natural market forces. That component can not be served by private and nongovernmental entities. It must be addressed, served, supported by government.

The concept of the public good really goes back much further than Smith, as anyone who has read Plato's *Republic* knows. It is a concept that is larger than individual well-being, a notion of a society that is greater than the well-being of certain individuals within it. In the expression, "the public good and the library's relationship to it," there is a vagueness, and this vagueness has

34

been something of a danger to us in the library field. We could very well spend a good deal of time debating about the definition of "public good." Anyone who has been in the library profession for even a fraction of the time I have has seen similar things happen. The semantic problem is one that we have grappled with for many decades as we addressed matters of policy and principle. We need to bypass semantic obstacles and develop a consensus and a focus—not a rigid definition—through which to integrate the activities of libraries with the public interest.

DEFINING THE ROLE OF LIBRARIES

There are elements of the public good upon which we can agree, but they have to do with our definitions of the role of libraries, our definitions of ALA's role, and our definitions of what is the appropriate relationship of this association to those elements. To state that we intend to forge coalitions for the public good is both an assertion and a challenge. It asserts that libraries do serve the public good and that they are more than simply utilitarian entities in our society. It asserts that the purposes served by libraries are at the root of the basic purposes of our society. It is central to our challenge that we attempt to link the goals and activities of our association with the most fundamental goals of the American people. In this regard, it is incumbent upon us to do something fairly dangerous, and that is to engage in an act of faith.

Addressing the relationship of libraries to the public good—not simply working within a fixed framework, but attempting to influence the structure of that framework—is very much a part of our responsibilities as members of the library profession. Whether one provides a narrow or broad definition of the library's role has a profound effect upon the kinds of services that it gives. Professor Kittredge at the Harvard Business School used to begin a course he taught each year by describing a particular business activity. It became immediately apparent to most of the class what subject he was talking about. He'd say, "What am I describing?" and they would reply, almost as one, "Railroads." He would then say, "No, transportation."

There are many definitions of what a library does. Most of them don't really incorporate the term "public good." Most of them speak of our functions. My suggestion is that those functions, important as they are, are really reflections of a larger purpose. The scope of that purpose influences in turn the functions that we feel are appropriate to our library organizations. A distinction also needs to be made between libraries and library organizations. I hope that we have learned from a decade and a half of debate over what constitutes a library issue, that there is a profound difference between an issue appropriate for the attention of a library, whether it is public, school, or academic, and what is an appropriate issue for a library association. Our individual libraries must be neutral, must be relatively apolitical and must be directly accountable to the political governmental structure of the communities they serve. We turn to our library association to address broad social issues that are beyond the appropriate sphere of interest and action of the individual library.

THE BROADER CONCERNS OF LIBRARIES

There is no question that what libraries do, in many people's minds, is provide and circulate books and provide access to information. Very few people, if asked "What does a library do?" would answer, "they safeguard basic democratic freedoms, they contribute to the quality of life in our society, they symbolize human aspirations, and they reflect the humanistic values that under lie our society." These are in fact essential social elements in the purpose of libraries. Libraries do not serve merely individual, informational, and recreational interests, but are part of the essential fabric of our society—its fragile cultural and social ecology.

Those social elements are central concerns of librarians responsible for efficiently and effectively providing the best service possible. But we come together as a national organization not only to find out how to better do what we have been doing, but to find out how we can influence the framework within which we function. We do more to reflect the framework of values in this society than to shape it. Libraries are limited in what they can do individually; they can't directly change the world or our society. But then, neither can environmentalists, or lawyers, or individual public policy groups. When brought together, however, these groups can have far more influence than can be realized by any one of them individually. When libraries come together as a national organization, our effectiveness in championing the cause of coalition building becomes self-evident.

I believe that there are alliances that we must strike in order to accomplish specific tasks, such as legislative lobbying. We know that it takes money to run libraries, and we know that if we go alone hat-in-hand to either the Congress or to legislators at the state and local levels, our influence is far less than if we approach them as an alliance. Alliances are crucial to success in the political sphere. However, if we are to approach other organizations to propose alliances for the public good, we must be prepared to assert a far more important role for the library. We must clearly define what we do and establish and assert the relationship of libraries to basic democratic freedoms, to the fundamental humanistic principles that are central to our very way of life. We also have to expect that potential partners in coalitions are going to say to us, "Well, what can you do for us?"

Let me go back to my earlier suggestion that what's crucial here is that we attempt to seek a consensus on a broader vision of what libraries do. We know that if we take any individual library, measure activities, seek a user study, and relate cost to benefit, we're going to come up with a very specific list of functions. When you put those specific functions together, the total adds up to something that is more than just a series of functions; the total adds up to a mission.

When libraries were founded in this country, the library profession was admired around the world as one that possessed a sense of mission, a sense of zeal, and a passion which became a movement. In the nineteenth century, the American library movement was very widely admired and imitated throughout the world. It's interesting to go back and read some of the statements that were made at the early gatherings of librarians in this country. More than a century ago, at what's usually considered to be the first national gathering of librarians, Charles C. Jewett announced to the assembled body: "We meet to provide for the diffusion of knowledge of good books." Well, that noble goal is one which we can respect in historical context, but I suspect that today Mr. Jewett's definition of the library's mission is not likely to gain us a great many coalition partners. We continue to attempt to foster an appreciation for good books, but during the course of this century, our profession has come a long way in creating a broader agenda.

Let me take a couple of areas that are very central to our mission. Intellectual freedom is one. I was very surprised, at one of the first ALA conferences I attended twenty years ago, to hear a debate over whether it was any of ALA's business if the federal government required librarians to take loyalty oaths as a condition of their employment. A great many members sitting there insisted that this was not the business of the ALA, that it was not our place to influence the thinking of government. If the law requires that there be loyalty oaths, then we should abide by that. Well, by a fairly narrow vote the ALA did agree that it was a library issue and that the ALA should go on record opposing the use of loyalty oaths as a condition of employment. To me, it was a very important step, and one that we've seen repeated again and again as part of a general recognition that an association concerned with intellectual freedom cannot limit its concern simply to attempting to prevent the censorship of books.

If the environment in which we function is not one that promotes the right of access, if we operate in a society in which the government practices secrecy, harassment, and censorship, then the efforts of individual institutions to safeguard intellectual freedom are largely futile.

Defense of intellectual freedom has been one of the great successes of the association, and our policy statements in the area of intellectual freedom are a testimony to it. We are concerned, as our statement on intellectual freedom and our Library Bill of Rights say, with rights of access to information anywhere in society, not just in libraries. We are concerned with the relationship of individuals to government and to information generated by government. We want and believe we must have a society in which democratic freedoms, such as the right of access to information, are safeguarded and guaranteed. We believe this, because, among other reasons, libraries need such a framework in order to function effectively. It is therefore the mission and purpose of the library to support those principles not just within individual libraries but in our society. If people are not free to associate; to gain access to neighborhoods, business establishments, or places of entertainment; if they can not buy a house because of their color or religion; all these restrictions have a deep and direct bearing on the way libraries operate in a democratic society.

We have broadened our definitions in other respects as well. We've come a long way in our concepts of information and informational services since the days of Charles C. Jewett. During my own time in this profession, our sense of the responsibility of libraries to the people we serve has changed quite radically, but perhaps still not as much as it needs to. We have not been as successful in this regard as in the area of intellectual freedom, but the potential is there for significant change. In our evolution, we have moved from institutions that respond only to demand, accepting as a given that those who already choose to use libraries are our primary clientele, to institutions that are sensitive to a wider audience.

LIBRARIES AS COALITION PARTNERS

Information is, of course, a dangerous entity in many regards. Ideas can be dangerous. We have moved from the simple provision of good books to recognizing the right and need of all people to gain access to whatever information they require in the pursuit of life, liberty, happiness, educational opportunity, and individual self-advancement. This is a right that we must defend; information that is related to everyday needs of survival is by no means less important than that which enhances academic advancement or intellectual edification. A central concern to libraries and the public good is the so-called "privitization of government information." Our concern with access to information has grown to the point where we must address governmental policies. Within the past three years, government has reduced by approximately twenty-five percent the number of titles available through the Government Printing Office. This is the topic that ALA's GODORT (Government Documents Round Table) has brought to our attention. Our government is making a concerted effort to transfer its responsibility for dissemination of information gathered at government (our) expense to the private sector.

When our government, by far the largest generator of information in our society, rejects its responsibility to provide that information, even to the point where it engages in a deliberate attempt to reduce access—for economic reasons or otherwise—then libraries can not be blind to the effects of these activities upon their mission. ALA must see that, however the public good is defined, it is in serious jeopardy when confronted with this challenge.

Do you for a second think that if we, as a body, marched down the street to the executive office building, our influence would be significant or successful in changing the present direction of government? Of course not. Information, particularly information generated by government, is not something generated for the benefit of libraries. Any threat to the free flow of information is a library issue, but it is of equal importance to a broad range of other organizations to which we must turn in attempting to build coalitions.

Here is where we have something extremely important to offer to potential coalition partners. There is hardly a group—whether it represents the interests of educational institutions, environmentalists, civil rights organizations, or cultural or social organizations—that isn't deeply dependent upon access to information. We, as potential partners in such coalitions, bring to that alliance something extremely important to those members. We have an informational specialty. Defining what we do in such terms can greatly improve ALA's appeal to potential coalition partners.

We were all delighted about the success of the referendum on the Detroit Public Library. That library is in one of the most economically hard hit sections of this country. However, despite government efforts to restrict funding, it was able to go directly to the people, and thus gain support denied by formal governmental appropriation. Important to this success is the history of the Detroit Public Library in building alliances within its community. An important aspect in the willingness of organizations throughout the Detroit metropolitan area to assist the Detroit Public Library is its contribution to the community. There is hardly a social or cultural agency in the city which has not come to have deep respect and gratitude to that institution for the role it has played in the development of information services. I can point to the efforts of Clara Jones and Bob Croneberger in developing information and referral services there, and more recently, to Jane Morgan, who helped build alliances specifically for the purpose of fostering public respect for and support of the public library. We've seen this kind of alliance building in many sectors of our society and I think the time has come when we must transfer what we've learned at the local level to the national level. But, we must do it not simply because libraries need something.

You may remember when the city council of Newark, New Jersey attempted a decade ago to close down the public library. The council actually did the library and all of us a favor because for years support for the library within the council had been gradually eroding. However, when the time finally came to say "Let's just wipe the library off the fiscal ledger," the public outcry against the move was phenomenal. Where did it come from? Not just from the pillars of the community and the friends of the library; it also came from ethnic minorities and people in the poorest segments of the community who said quite clearly to the city council, "We look upon the library as a symbol of hope, of the possibility of raising ourselves up out of conditions of poverty. The library is extremely important, more important than most of the other things that you want to spend money on." It is a great success story, and the Newark Public Library has improved since that time.

When the function of libraries is put in terms of their contributions to the community, people see their centrality. The challenge to us is to continue to help them see it in those terms, to describe our larger purposes. We must assert that libraries are central to the quality of life in our society, that libraries have a direct role in preserving democratic freedoms. Free access to information and the opportunity of every individual to improve his or her mind, employment prospects, and lifestyle are fundamental rights in this society.

It would be a mistake for us to conclude that the problems we face in obtaining funding and support at the federal level are caused by some trickery, some evil but brilliant individuals who have seized control of government and are thwarting the will of the public. Sometimes that *is* what's happening, but we should recognize that our society is somewhat schizophrenic—no one wants to pay taxes but everyone wants a great society.

The historical pendulum swings at different times, and different elements come into play. Many of you will remember that in the 1960s there was enormous enthusiasm and idealism in this association. Many of you were part of the battles waged and debates held on the social mission of libraries. I think it's important for us to see the cyclical nature of things. What we saw in the sixties was a reaction against the complacency of the fifties. What we may be seeing now is a reaction to the sixties. It may be a stronger reaction than expected, but I do believe that it is a part of a cycle. Despite certain successes of the sixties, the expansion of the cultural mission of libraries into a more socially oriented one came a bit too late. I am speaking primarily in economic terms. There was money available in the sixties to help change the nature of communities; much of the money that went to model cities, day-care centers, and other great society programs might well have been spent on library programs if librarians in the fifties had been planning ahead.

Right now, the government seems to be saying "the public good is simply a big fence and a big army. Government has no business concerning itself with poverty, or suffering, or the quality of life." Some of you may think those are not library issues. But can we really ignore the effects of poverty and discrimination, frustration and despair? Major social issues are related to the purposes of our institutions, and even more pragmatically, they are related to any possibility of success in fulfilling our mission. We have to do what we can to try to influence the actions and attitudes of our government by joining with other groups—by building coalitions. We've had some successes. We have helped to forestall or in some instances turn around actions of the government to impose secrecy or restraint upon information dissemination. We have had some small but nonetheless significant influence upon positions taken at the Government Printing Office and at the Office of Management and Budget. However, they are not enormous successes and therein lies the danger. We may become frustrated that the success is so small. Then we must remember that the fifties did become the sixties. People are one day going to grow tired of hearing that the national purpose is to do less; that the national purpose is to build a big army and that anyone outside of the army or of private big business is not the concern of government.

There is no guarantee that by 1991 the country is going to turn around again, that hope and idealism and a desire to recreate a sense of national purpose will return. I do say to you "what do we have to lose by assuming it is a possibility?" And what do we have to gain by assuming the future has no place for libraries? It may be a gamble, but the very creation of libraries in this country was an act of faith. Through the broadening of our mission over the years, we've profoundly increased the contribution that we make to the public good. We must help to shape the framework of social values and not simply respond to it.

The Library's Role in a Multicultural Society
Virginia Hamilton

I am a writer who is every day involved in expressing through my fiction those qualities that make created characters relevant to the interests and ideals of a humanistic society. In the nonfiction work I have done, I've documented the deeds of talented individuals, relating their lives and works to the times through which they lived and to a social order which at its best expresses democratic ideals as fundamental to its citizens' existence. I travel often, talking to librarians, teachers, and students all over the country and in Canada about those connections that make us all part of the same concern for the public good, not only in terms of my field of literature for young people, but in education, literacy, free expression, and free access to information.

My purpose as a novelist and biographer has been to portray as clearly as possible the essence of the black community and culture, its history and traditions, in order to demonstrate the nexus the one group has with other groups. It is our humanity with which I am concerned, and through literature, I endeavor to bring to all people the best of my heritage.

The Afro-American historian Carter Woodson wrote: "If a race has no history, if it has no worthwhile tradition, it becomes a negligible factor in the thought of the world and it stands in danger of being exterminated."

The truth of this statement as it applies to ethnic groups has been made chillingly clear in the present through the shattered lives of dying Ethiopians; in recent history, when Hitlerism denied a Semitic people their dignity, their life, their liberty, and their history; and in earlier times, when black Africans were forced into bondage, whereby they lost most of their history and traditions as well as their freedom.

Whenever individuals are denigrated because of their ideas, color, or religion, or because they are poor and deprived, you can be sure that those individuals are in danger of becoming less than human in the eyes of the world, of becoming non-beings.

In the 1950s, McCarthyism helped to make non-beings out of many ordinary citizens as well as great artists and leaders. Dissident organizations and individuals were discredited. Public access to information about international events and national policy was controlled. Through an aberration termed *guilt-by-association*, many individuals were blacklisted and shunned. They lost their jobs, and for years they were unable to work.

Senator Joseph McCarthy hoped to achieve power by exploiting defense issues surrounding the cold war and the fear of Communists in our government. He sent two assistants to Europe "to track down and destroy 'subversive' literature [such as the works of Emerson and Thoreau] in libraries of the American Information Service. . . ."

Black leaders such as W. E. B. Du Bois and the great Paul Robeson had works by and about them removed from library stacks. Even Du Bois' beloved Atlanta University, where he taught for ten years, saw fit to move his work to vaults to avoid government interference.

As the director of the Peace Information Agency, Dr. Du Bois was indited in 1951 by a Washington grand jury and put on trial as an " 'agent' of a foreign principal" because of his international work for peace and his progressive politics. Although he was later acquitted of all charges, he was "smeared" as being sympathetic to communism and he was denied a passport for six years. He was furthermore denied his livelihood.

Dr. Du Bois said this about his situation then:

> The white world which had never liked me but was forced in the past to respect me, now ignored me or deliberately distorted my work. A whispering campaign continually intimated that some hidden treason or bribery could be laid at my door if the government had not been lenient. . . I bowed before the storm. But I did not break . . . I lost my leadership of my race. . . The colored children ceased to hear my name.

Paul Robeson also lost his place as one of our most esteemed Americans, much honored, a star of stage and screen, an idol of millions, whose magnificent voice was highly praised in this country and the world over. Robeson was the first American black to become an overwhelmingly popular success in his own country, among all races. But he fell from grace because of his so-called leftist politics and friends in that Cold War period.

Carl Rowen, a journalist who later became director of the United States Information Agency, wrote in *Ebony* magazine in 1957, six years after Robeson's passport had been revoked, that Robeson had been a tragic figure "regarded by some as a casualty in the Cold War":

> Whatever the reasons, for all practical purposes, Paul Robeson's voice is silent today. The great concert impressarios pretend he no longer exists. City officials padlock public halls at the mere rumor that he is coming. Hollywood wouldn't touch him with a long-armed geiger counter... Autograph seekers who once trailed his every step have dropped by the wayside to make room for FBI agents. Newspapers that once carried rave notices of his magnificent talents now run only an occasional item...

When I began work in 1969 gathering research for a Du Bois biography, some of his twenty-five books, long out of print, were at last being reissued. Public information on Paul Robeson, whose biography I wrote two years after the Du Bois book was published, was much more difficult to come by. Material which should have been available on microfilm and in hard copy was often not to be found. However, through my publishers, unpublished doctoral theses were made available to me covering Robeson's career in the theater, in motion pictures, and on the concert stage, as well as on his early nationalist years. The British writer Marie Seton, an old friend of Mr. Robeson, kindly gave me permission to use material on him for which she was the sole source.

It is important to note that by the time the biographies on Dr. Du Bois and Paul Robeson were published (*W. E. B. Du Bois: A Biography* in 1972 and *Paul Robeson, The Life and Times of a Free Black Man* in 1974), Du Bois had been dead for almost ten years and Robeson was in full retirement and died soon after. By this time, a generation of Americans did not know who these men were; they had never heard their names nor understood their contributions. This is still the case for segments of the population. But I am happy to say that both biographies are now in print. These two titles and much other Robeson and Du Bois material can again be found in libraries.

Young people entering college today were a year old when the apostle of nonviolence, the Reverend Martin Luther King, was shot and killed. Without free information concerning this man, without books in print and periodicals, without libraries, it is not inconceivable that a college freshman might say, "I've heard the name, let's see, isn't he a holiday? But I'm not sure what he's known for—just who was he, anyway?" This sounds like fiction. It's a sad prospect, unbelievable, as shocking as it was to me when I was asked, "Who is Paul Robeson?" But believe it when I tell you there are college students who don't remember or don't know Selma, Montgomery, and Little Rock, or Rosa Parks and James Meredith. They might have been absent from government or history class during the hour the teacher covered the civil rights movement—units on black history are usually gone through fairly quickly in most integrated high schools.

There was a time in this world when the griots of Africa remembered the past for their people, when bards and minstrels of Europe kept the Arthurian and Breton traditions through story-songs. Scholars of the Middle Ages and Renaissance used a system of historical memorization which called for "the attachment of each piece of information to a decoration, tableau, or piece of furniture within a visualized "memory palace," which could be as simple as a single room or as complex as an entire town, containing thousands of rooms." Our libraries are also memory palaces.

I believe in the importance of past and present Afro-American life and history and culture to the multi-ethnic fabric of our society and in the necessity of making them known to all Americans. I believe in preserving the documentary history of that life in libraries for succeeding American generations, lest we forget who was a Martin King, who was a Paul Robeson.

I have written twenty books, fiction and non-fiction, and not one of them could have been completed without the free use of, and access to, information from public and university libraries.

My love of books and libraries goes back a considerable way. Growing up poor and black on the edge of the Great Depression, it is rather strange, I think, that I grew up in a house full of books. My mother came from a farming family; my father had been a musician, a classical mandolinist. A graduate of Iowa State Business School, he and his partner were founders of a black newspaper that quickly went broke. But Kenneth Hamilton did have quite successful mandolin clubs around the country that in 1903 were integrated—male and female, black and white.

My father was a great storyteller and reader. There were not huge numbers of books in our house, but what we had were choice— all of Poe, lots of O. Henry stories, Maupassant, and essays of Montaigne. There were pamphlets, magazines such as *Life* and the *Saturday Evening Post*, and the *New Yorker*—Dad loved the cosmopolitan *New Yorker* stories. Works by Du Bois were in the bookcase in the livingroom and *Crisis* magazine, the official organ of the NAACP, of which Du Bois was the founding editor and quite often a contributor, came to our house periodically. *Crisis* magazine often printed marvelous messages from around the world, such as this one in its 1929 issue: "Let not the 12 million Negroes be ashamed of the fact that they are the grandchildren of slaves. There is no dishonour in being slaves. There is dishonour in being slave-owners. Let us realize that the future is with those who would be truthful, pure and loving. For, as the old wise men have said, truth ever is, untruth never was. . ." This is part of a letter from Mohandas Gandhi to American blacks.

I grew up in the village of Yellow Springs, Ohio, where Antioch College made Horace Mann its president in 1854. Mann was known by then as the "father of the American public school." He pioneered the concept of universal education that would be non-sectarian and free. A Unitarian, he had been attacked and became famous for barring sectarian religious publications from Boston's schools in 1843. Mann's law partner from Boston, Moncure Conway, a southerner from Virginia, was inspired by Mann and moved to Cincinnati, Ohio, where he promptly became a staunch abolitionist. Moncure Conway freed his father's Virginia slaves and under armed guard brought them by train to Yellow Springs where he established a colony for them. So it was that Yellow Springs became the inspirational home for fugitives and abolitionists alike.

Horace Mann died in Yellow Springs in 1859, about the time that my grandfather, Levi Perry, travelled the dangerous Underground Railroad as a fugitive from slavery.

Before he died, Grandpa Perry is said to have talked quite a lot about his escape from bondage with the aid of abolitionist John Rankin, who helped some 2,000 fugitives and was for decades a force for freedom. Rankin and his wife, Jean Lowry, lived with their nine sons and four daughters in a house on a bluff high above the Ohio River. As many as twelve escapees were secreted in the Rankin house at one time. And the Rankins were ever proud not to have lost a single "passenger" on the Underground.

The Rankin home at Ripley, Ohio, is now a historical memorial. Every spring, my Uncle Kingsley Perry made the pilgrimage with his family to the Rankin House "just to visit," he would say. He never talked much about it. But making the trip was something he obviously felt compelled to do.

Growing up in a community where individualists have been and continue to be an inspiration to me, it is probably not unusual that the small village library became the focus of my childhood. For it held for me all of the possibilities in the world beyond my village. Twice a week, one mad individualist we called the Story Lady came to school, rain or shine, to deliver our class to the fieldstone library where we were allowed to take out four to six books each. Like a stone cottage, the library was, with gables and eaves that brought to mind the gingerbread house out of "Hansel and Gretel." But it was far more pleasant within.

The Story Lady—I don't think I ever knew her real name, but that was her real name to us—kept us occupied on the short walk from school with her extraordinary observations of the ordinary life around us. I remember one day we had gone out after an ice storm. The Story Lady pointed out all of the sparrows sitting still on the telephone lines. We saw that, but did not think much of it until she told us to look again, more closely. Only then did we take the time to squint, to notice that each one of the little birds was encased in its own little ice shroud. Tiny birds' feet were frozen to the telephone wires, the Story Lady said. "They're straight up and down dead up there," she told us in no uncertain terms. "When that ice melts in the sun, they'll go plop, plop, plop to the ground." We gazed in awe at the gruesome spectacle. I never forgot the sight, or that afternoon.

I don't know how many of us went back that day after school to see if the little sparrows had plopped. I know I did. And they had. That was what was so wonderful about my beloved Story Lady, who was our one and only town librarian. She always told us the truth, whether through fiction or fact.

Years later, I used that memory almost as it happened in a book called *Arilla Sun Down* in a winter scene after an ice storm. However, I would have much more than this odd happening for which to thank the good Lady.

She shepherded us into the fieldstone library and to a flight of stairs that led us down to the basement. As we went down, she had us touch the stone walls. "See, the warmth of summer is still in the stone." And so it was. Here it was the dead of winter and we pondered the mystery of nature that could hold onto the sun deep in its rock.

In the basement, we sat comfortably on a pattern rug in front of a huge furnace. Here, the Story Lady settled before us and read us stories. I don't know if you can imagine the scene. We were all children once; we each have an extraordinary memory of something from that time. The simple feeling of the closeness of the world came into the shadow-filled basement chamber where the Story Lady had our full attention. The only sounds were the quiet sighing of the furnace and the steady sound of her voice as she read us all manner of stories—Jack tales, ghost tales, adventure tales. That time around the furnace is my first clear recollection of my love of books and libraries. It was there in the basement of the library that I first heard tales about John Henry, Robin Hood, Sleepy Hollow, Daniel Boone, the Indian Uncle Saynday stories and the "Story About Ping," set in China.

The Story Lady believed, apparently, that all children—even we, who were rather good readers—could and must read and be read to. Her mission was to show us the lovely shape and substance of the English language.

My appetite for reading has never ceased. The good Lady easily reinforced what took place in my home environment, for it was my good luck to have descended from a slew of talkers and story-tellers, plain out-and-out liars at times, who didn't only tell stories but created fictions when they forgot parts of real stories or family history, or when the real family stories got a bit stale; who, in effect, created who they were and where they came from and what they would become through acts of imagination. Their persistence in perpetuating our history through story-telling, by influencing me, is why I write story after story in order to discover where the truth begins or even where it is. I search out the truth, and libraries give me the documentation and resources to give greater depth and meaning to my work.

I became a student of black history at the age of twelve after reading Shirley Graham's *There Was Once a Slave*, a biography of the life of Frederick Douglass, a book that literally changed my life and thought and enabled me years later to find a way to work through what I term "living biography" in presenting the lives and times of two great men.

In writing a recent novel entitled *Junius Over Far*, half of which takes place on a fictional and remote Caribbean island, I made use of my local public library and college library resources.

The novel is an adventure tale about a young man's love for his grandfather and the relationship between black and white descendants of a slave-owning family on a now ruined, back island sugar plantation.

In the local libraries, I investigated material concerning the African slave trade to the West Indies, Carib Indian peoples, Caribbean island flora and fauna, the United States Coast Guard, West Indian migrations and populations, West Indian migration to the United States, West Indian colloquial speech and languages, island governments, buccaneers and pirates, the climate of the Caribbean Sea, Caribbean Sea sailing lanes, and leisure uses for fishing and sailing vessels. I was familiar with the area that I would fictionalize; therefore, I could experience some of my research. Moreover, the bibliography of one text led me to several others. It was important for me to know as much as possible about all of the subjects I have listed, even though only limited amounts of the research were utilized in the final book.

It is quite an unbelievable sight to watch Coast Guard cutters suddenly appear out of nowhere, coming up a tropic bay, dispatching men in thirty-foot rubber rafts along the way in a swift and powerful enforcement assignment. Combining observation and firsthand experience with research allows the author to write a fiction with enough authority to make it thoroughly believable.

We carry our histories, our pasts, around with us in the present through states of mind, family history, and historical fact. In order to pass on to others whatever knowledge I have gained about my history and culture, I often experiment with artistic forms other than fiction, such as biography. Recently, I became interested in finding a way to present very old American black folktales, many of which molder away in texts of microscopic print or in project manuscripts. I felt that, if presented properly, young people as well as adults would find these folktales a pleasure to read. But first I had to uncover the variety of original material that I knew must be there even though we hear mostly about the animal tales when we think of American black folktales. The animal tales are only a part of the total material.

Many of the early collectors attempted to record the material as they heard it or thought they heard it. The result was often a fractured, hardly readable English more or less in the manner of Joel Chandler Harris' rendering of his Uncle Remus offerings. What I hoped to do was to retell the real black folktales in a narrative form that would evoke the feeling and style of the original tellers, many of whom were slaves, some of whom were my ancestors.

Fortunately, only nine miles from my home, back in the hills, is the small historic black community of Wilberforce, Ohio, where Wilberforce University and Central State University are situated side by side. Wilberforce University is an African Methodist Episcopal Church school founded in 1856. In 1894, fresh from his studies at the University of Berlin, W. E. B. Du Bois came to Wilberforce to teach Latin, German, and Greek. The much newer Central State University is the only state-assisted black university in Ohio. Central State has 2,500 students and a wonderful higher education library, plus special collections of black materials that one would be hard-pressed to find anywhere else in a library of its size.

The director of the library, Dr. G. T. Johnson, said about it: "We project our collection in such a fashion that it will reflect not only the institution's offerings but also, a body of works dealing with black people wherever black people have lived." The library serves both Central and Wilberforce and surrounding communities. It began its collection of black materials in the early days of Wilberforce University.

The special collection has 8,000 volumes written by and about blacks. Three other collections in a micro-format augment this collection, including 1,236 titles of doctoral dissertations written by and about blacks; 12,000 titles of the Atlanta University Library black cultural collection, which includes some of the Du Bois Atlanta Studies in Race Relations; the American Missionary Association Archives dealing specifically with that period when the association played a vital role in the establishment of black institutions, particularly in the South; WPA project slave narratives for Ohio; Paul Lawrence Dunbar papers from 1872 to 1906; Charles W. Chestnut papers; and the register of blacks in Ohio counties from 1804 to 1861. Central State Library also has an African library collection consisting of 992 pieces dealing with the slave trade and abolition in France and Africa. I used the rare volumes of the Central State University Library collection for some of my folktale research. My completed volume of tales is entitled *The People Could Fly: American Black Folktales.*

Historically, we Americans have thought of ourselves as deeply egalitarian. Egalitarianism is stronger in some more than others, it is true, but all of us are aware at least of a constant assertion of the equality of all. We have proposed a unique concept, that the youngest among us have the right to books that reflect their cultural and racial heritage. Cultural democracy is a giant step on the way to equal education and the first principle to the attainment of human equality. Underlying it is the assumption that non-whites, although different, are as important, as human, and as American as whites. I make the further assumption that all people have the right to free access to information about themselves and their past. This is so important to people who are continually cut off from their history. My book of folktales serves to demonstrate that storytelling is not merely a thing of the past, but a continuing cultural imperative, illuminating the triumphs of talking and telling among the people in the present, and revealing the connections of blacks to their historical past.

Here is what Dr. Johnson at The Central State University Library had to say about the college students who he meets through his work: "The average student who comes to Central State comes from an integrated society, from schools that are typical in the sense that black history and black culture play no part in an integrated setting." Continued Dr. Johnson:

It was one of Malcolm X's great fears about an integrated society that it would cause us to lose our culture. While those who deal with young people in a lower education setting may not see that, we see that every day here at the university. Very often, a student comes to us and is given an assignment to write on some black person. One of the approaches we at the library use is to find out where the student comes from. And it's likely that we can come up with a well-known name associated with that place. Very often, though, we are so disappointed that the youngster doesn't know the black history of the area in which he or she lives. A student from Chicago won't have heard of Jean Baptise Pointe DuSable (who created the foundations of Chicago) or a student from here won't know anything about Paul Lawrence Dunbar, born nearby in Dayton, Ohio.

It is sad to realize that if blacks are deprived of their heritage, whites will not know of it either; and therefore, that heritage, that knowledge, is rendered insignificant to both groups.

Dr. Johnson and his staff, and the unique Central State University Library, satisfy an enormous need for those who do not know and need to learn. One might say that such a library system, whose director is a humanist who keeps the interests and desires of his constituency ever in mind, guarantees that those who do not know have a place in which to find the information that will allow them to educate themselves about themselves. It would be a grave disservice to the community and an injustice to a most vulnerable group if present economic difficulties cause the Central State Library to curtail its services.

Quality library services are of the utmost importance for the most economically deprived among us. But we are all being deprived when libraries can no longer acquire a broad base of materials. Moreover, incidents in the present are symptomatic; they are chilling reminders of the repressive times of the 1950s. Free access to information has become suspect, as groups cry, "filth" and "secular humanism," and demand that books they single out should be removed from library shelves.

As a member of the Author's League, I, with seven other authors of books for youths, including Madeleine L'Engle, Milton Meltzer, and William Steig, protested in writing to the Peoria Board of Education the Peoria school district's decision to ban from elementary school libraries three books by Judy Blume. We asked the Peoria board to rescind its decision. We stated that such actions "teach a poor lesson, one of intolerance, distrust, and contempt for the values protected by the First Amendment." We stated that the board's rationale, to stop children below the seventh grade from reading the books, "deprives older students of access in their school libraries to books . . . 'fit' for them to read and reduces the level of library reading fare for all students to a level the board deems acceptable for the youngest student."

A month later, the school board voted to restore the Blume books "upon condition that the administration develop a procedure to limit access to older children. Any student who has parental permission, regardless of age, will have access to them."

Since I am a writer of literature for children and young adults, it is the banning of these kinds of books that I am most familiar with. However, the Peoria case is not at all an isolated incident. These often-successful attempts to censor our reading are more insidious and more dangerous to the public good and the public welfare than at first seems evident.

I consider myself a humanist and a student of human nature and human affairs. I stand before you as the best testimony I know of in defense of free access to information for all, particularly the poor and deprived. Growing up in rural Ohio, learning in an integrated country school almost nothing concerning the racial group to which I belonged, it was through the public library in that quaint fieldstone cottage that I discovered there was a moving picture of history, literature, and life that included my life and my people and that I might see by taking out a book from the library and opening it. I, an author, am one who writes books. You are the ones who have charge of books. Together, we form a fellowship, a coalition for the welfare of all.

BIBLIOGRAPHY

Antiochiana, "Horace Mann," Antioch College Library, Yellow Springs, Ohio.

Aptheker, Herbert, ed., *A Documentary History of the Negro People in the United States.* 4 vols. (New York: The Citadel Press, 1974).

——— , *The Autobiography of W. E. B. Du Bois.* (New York: International Publishers, 1968).

Bennett, Jr., Lerone, *Before the Mayflower: A History of Black America* (Chicago: Johnson Publishing Company, Inc., 1961), p. 357.

"Blume Books Restricted in Peoria, Ill.; Five Titles Banned In Hanover, Pa." *SLJ School Library Journal,* New York: R.R. Bowker Co., January, 1985.

Du Bois, W. E. B., *In Battle for Peace,* With Comments By Shirley Graham (New York: Masses & Mainstream, 1952).

Graham, Shirley, *There Was Once a Slave* (New York: Messner, 1947).

Hamilton, Virginia, *Junius Over Far* (New York: Harper & Row Publishers, 1985).

——— , *Paul Robeson.* (New York: Harper & Row Publishers, 1974).

——— , *W. E. B. Du Bois, A Biography* (New York: T. Y. Crowell Company, 1972).

Hamilton, ed., *The Writings of W. E. B. Du Bois* (New York: T. Y. Crowell Company, 1975), p. 217.

Hofstadter, Richard, *The Paranoid Style in American Politics* (New York: Alfred A. Knopf, 1965).

Morison, Samual Eliot, Henry Steele Commager, and William E. Leuchtenburg, *The Growth of the American Republic. Vol. II* (London: Oxford University Press, 1967), p. 681.

Ploski, Harry A. and Roscoe C. Brown, Jr., compilers and eds., *The Negro Almanac* (New York: Bellwether Publishing Company, Inc., 1967).

Rowen, Carl, in *Ebony* Magazine, Chicago: The Johnson Publishing Company, October 1957.

Spence, Jonathan D., "The Memory Palace of Mateo Rici." The *New Yorker* Magazine, June 1985, p. 121.

Woodson, Carter, in interview with the Director, Dr. Johnson (quote on display). Wilberforce, Ohio: The Hallie Q. Brown Memorial Library Black Collection, The Central State University.

PART TWO
Issues in Defining the Public Good

The Awesome Mission of Library Leadership in America

Major R. Owens

Our leadership has an awesome burden upon its shoulders. The library profession is at a pivotal point. This decade is a decisive one for all groups and individuals related in one way or another to the information-service sector. In this age of information, the recognition of the power of information is growing, and the business of library and information services has been perceived as too critical to be left only to library professionals. Powerful intruding forces threaten to obliterate the influence of the library profession. To avoid becoming obsolete, we must not only act decisively; we must also act swiftly.

To perform effectively in this age, we must sharply define our professional tasks. We must reach a consensus on critical aspects of national information policy and on how national information resources can best be structured. We must make new efforts to develop and finance a more systematic approach to the training and grooming of library leadership. From recruiting library students, to developing post-graduate seminars and management internships, there is so much more to be done.

The very fortunate accidents of history which produced Melvil Dewey, Constance Winchell, Emerson Greenaway, L. Quincy Mumford, Frances Henney, Clara Jones, and Thomas Galvin may not be repeated in the future. The mission forced upon library leadership requires more leaders who are giants. Some giants are born; some giants are made; but all giants perform better in a supportive environment that consciously nurtures their efforts.

Librarians cannot measure up to the challenge they face without strong, creative leadership. Leaders must set priorities; leaders

59

must establish professional strategies; leaders must define the tasks and mobilize the resources involved in accomplishing our goals.

But who will create a sympathetic public environment to permit librarianship to flourish? Who will allocate the resources to implement programs recommended by numerous workshops, round tables, task force groups and other professional bodies? How will we exert a reasonable degree of influence on those who are responsible for making the decisions about resources?

MAKING CRITICAL DECISIONS AND CREATING A STRATEGY

Landmark events which will shape our future are occurring now. Where once our profession was permitted to quietly reign, powerful forces have invaded the turf of librarians. They issue memos, regulations, and mandates that threaten our autonomy. Library professional activities which lend credibility to certain providers of information; the ALA designation of vehicles and instruments for compiling, editing, and packaging reference information; the development of classification schemes, descriptive cataloging, and other standardized processes; the formulation of policies on the dissemination of government information; the refinement of bibliographic certifications and evaluations; these are only a few of the important, far-reaching tasks over which the organized profession has in the past exercised great and sometimes nearly total influence.

But now this influence is threatened, and one of the most powerful of these threats, the Reagan administration's Office of Management and Budget, is seeking to drive professional librarians from all significant decision-making positions within the executive branch of the federal government. And, of course, this administration has chosen to make—without the advice and participation of librarians—some very far-reaching decisions on federal publications policies and the overall management of federal information resources.

The parallel attack on the credentials of professional librarians by the federal Office of Personnel Management is not a chance or happenstance occurrence. There is clearly a well coordinated group within the Reagan Administration which is determined to shape the contours of the age of information, particularly as it relates to government information. And this group views organized librarians as a major obstacle to its agenda.

Non-governmental forces, less powerful and less overtly hostile, are seeking to mold the age of information in ways which guarantee maximum profits. The information industry continues its misguided alliance with the Reagan administration's "library hit squads." The ironic and unfortunate results for these budding private-sector groups will be fewer reliable sources from which they may extract their raw material. A partnership between the library profession and the information industry would yield meaningful results for all groups.

Attempts to push librarians to the periphery of decision-making are taking place right now. Librarians must buttress their mainstream role immediately or they will lose it. The ball is presently still in our hands; the initiative still belongs to us. But if we stumble or if we fumble, the ball will be lost. Opportunists will seize the initiative. Librarians should listen to the time-honored advice of William Shakespeare (Julius Caesar; Act IV, Scene 3):

> There is a tide in the affairs of men which taken at the flood leads on to fortune; omitted, all the voyage of their life is bound in shallows and in miseries. On such a full sea are we now afloat, and we must take the current when it serves, or loose our venture.

In every sphere of librarianship, at every level and in every type of library, the tide must be taken at the flood.

Have we decided, for example, how the use of library and media centers should be incorporated into elementary and junior high school curriculums? What will we do to guarantee that those who have the power will appropriate money to put adequate libraries in every school, and place in each such library a professional librarian? What more will librarians do to ensure that every high school graduate will be exposed to the research training they need to utilize college, university, or public libraries competently? How will librarians act in concert to guarantee that all college students graduate with a high degree of information literacy, the kind of literacy which will enable them to use information with ease in their daily work?

And, among these new professionals, how will librarians conduct themselves in order to create an enthusiastic, permanent constituency for library and information services, a constituency which does not take the utility and convenience of their libraries for granted? How do we make this articulate group of users more supportive and more effective in mobilizing library resources? What will we do to inspire them to lead the way in setting budget priorities to benefit library and information services, and in raising taxes when necessary.

And how will we create new systems or refine old systems and networks to draw on the proliferating multitude of sources—automated and manual—to provide maximum universal access at the lowest possible costs? What federal, regional, and state information networks should we work to create? How can public libraries be transformed into information powerhouses for average citizens, learning centers where the whole family can have its information needs met?

None of these questions or problems should be left for other groups or professions to answer or resolve for us. Librarians must take the tide at the flood. And the good news for library leaders is that as they take the tide they will find many good sailing ships for the trip. The good news is that we have the blueprints, the reports, the models, and the checklists. We have the reports and commissioned papers from the National Commission on Library and Information Services. We have the deliberations of the Joint Committee on Printing. We have reports from the last White House Conference on Libraries; we have state plans; we have almost all of the master-plans and proposals we may ever need.

The tragedy is that our abundant knowledge and paper plans are not enough. The need is for focus, for concentration, for a central guiding strategy. Library leaders must construct an appropriate set of dominoes. Before we mobilize our power to carry out a strategy, our leaders must identify which actions deserve priority and in what sequence they should be initiated.

If librarians are to be the commanders in the mainstream of activities related to libraries and information services, we must have a well designed steering mechanism. We have the advantage of being anchored by a set of time-honored principles, processes, and procedures. We have met the challenges of the past. Our problem is the stormy, unfamiliar, changing sea of the present. We must begin by setting forth and emphasizing a few pivotal theories and positions to guide us through the waters which now surround us.

GUIDELINES FOR THE FUTURE

Position 1: The library profession alone is qualified to effectively cope with the information explosion in this age. No other group is equipped to guide us in the mainstream of activities related to library and information services.

If the library profession did not exist, it would have to be invented. Despite the fact that society presently refuses to recognize this, librarians still have the duty to conduct themselves under the assumption that librarians and libraries are vital cement in the structure of our civilization. A full understanding and acceptance of this position by librarians everywhere would raise the profession to a new level of pride and profundity. Practicing librarians would be less likely to be overwhelmed by the trivia of their daily tasks. Regardless of the work limitations at any one moment, the broader vision and goals would continue to provide stimulation, inspiration, and a sense of direction.

Of even greater importance is the fact that such a firmly held and strongly articulated position would serve as a beginning bulwark against the intruding forces which seek to manipulate library and information policies to serve vested interests. This declaration of the library profession's vital necessity in the age of information is a crucial step in the process of staking out the "turf" which belongs to us. We must proclaim ourselves the premier experts, the final authority on matters related to library and information services. Just as doctors insist on their omnipotence in medical affairs, and lawyers, without question, assume their role as the final interpreters of the law, librarians must not hesitate or equivocate. Constructive arrogance is clearly one of the qualities needed for the success of any profession.

Position 2: The definition and execution of the librarian's mission cannot be separated from considerations of education and certification requirements, salaries, fringe benefits, and working conditions.

The failure to insist on reasonable classification structures and the failure to enforce standards leaves our professional doors wide open to a polyglot body of less qualified information workers. The failure to adopt a more aggressive national stance on salaries, benefits, and working conditions erodes the foundation of the profession.

It is not by accident that the professions which have the highest income—lawyers, doctors, accountants—also have the greatest control over the education, certification, and working conditions of their members. It is useless to debate the question of which came first—the control or the higher income. And it is equally pointless to discuss whether income or the status is more important. All of these factors are inextricably interwoven and they are also fluid, forever changing as larger societal forces change. The history of the accounting profession will show that its power and influence has greatly escalated within the last three decades as the public demand for greater accountability from private as well as public entities has increased.

What should be most troubling to our library leadership is the fact that as the demand for our services in the age of information increases, attempts to lessen our influence and negate our power are also increasing. To reverse this trend, to rally to meet this challenge, is at the heart of library leadership in America.

Position 3: The present paucity of public commitment and available resources must not be allowed to smother creative conceptions of the kind of information services which libraries should provide. Blueprints, grand designs, and legislative programs should not be shelved as impractical merely because the present environment is shallow and restrictive.

While we have no choice but to operate at the levels provided by present budgets and authority, we still have an obligation to plan, advocate, and agitate for the ideal services that we know are needed.

As our decision makers are aroused and awakened to the necessities of the information age, we must have answers, solutions, and plans to place before them. A broad understanding of the mechanisms needed to utilize the power of information is inevitable. As the demand for library services intensifies, the profession must be prepared. And at the point when legislators are ready to act, we must have a program to set before them; it will be too late for studies, surveys, and pilot projects.

One grand example of this kind of preparedness is the national legislative planning checklist. (We could call this collection of outlined proposals the Legislative Fantasies of the First Librarian in Congress.) These items represent the kind of federal umbrella of support activities which we could undertake at the state and local levels:

a. A massive increase in aid to library education

b. Federal subsidies for long-term protection against rising postal and telecommunications rates

c. Continuation of LSCA with funding at the pre-1981 levels plus a one-time capital grant program for new technology hardware

d. A national designation of library and information services as a public utility important for national security

e. Legislation to insure the availability of certain data bases, retrieval systems, and collections in the interest of national security

f. Federal monitoring and supervision of nationwide information systems

g. Requirements for more streamlined management of federal information resources-executive branch libraries and government documents from all sources

h. Decentralization of the Library of Congress

The three pivotal positions enumerated above must be given full attention if we are to set the mission of library leadership on its proper course and if we are to make that mission manageable.

FORGING COALITIONS WITHIN THE PROFESSION

The success of our library leadership is very much dependent on the ability of that leadership to stimulate, inspire, and unite the rest of us. A profession under attack must, at least temporarily, become a movement. E. J. Josey has set in motion a process of forging coalitions with numerous other groups, and we must place new energy behind this effort. But before we move forward to forge grand coalitions with all of the groups who belong to the information sector, let us first create solidarity among all of those who carry the title of librarian.

In this effort we may be guided by the spirit of Matthew Arnold in his poem, *Dover Beach*:

Ah, love, let us be true
to one another! For the world, which seems
to lie before us like a land of dreams,
so various, so beautiful, so new,
hath really neither joy, nor love, nor light,
nor certitude, nor peace, nor help for pain,
and we are here as on a darkling plane
swept with confused alarms of struggle and flight
where ignorant armies clash by night.

Librarians, let us be true to one another. Children's librarians, unite with adult librarians; school libraries, join hands with university librarians; medical librarians, meet law librarians. Catalogers, reference librarians, film librarians, federal librarians, special librarians, church and synagogue librarians, military librarians—all must pause for a moment to be recognized by each other. Branch librarians, chief librarians, professors of library science, state librarians, the Librarian of Congress—all must focus their minds on shaping a common future.

Librarians, let us be true to one another. Before we move to coalesce with others, we must remember to act among ourselves to create a critical mass. The numbers are great enough; the first element of the critical mass is in place. Even if we mobilize only those information professionals who are librarians, our numbers are great enough. But to be a critical mass, we must be moving in the same direction. And furthermore, to be able to command attention and achieve a meaningful impact, we must move with emotional intensity, with vigor, with great fervor. Librarians can fully command their domain and remain at the core of decision making if they believe it is possible.

A critical mass is like a giant snowball rolling down a hill. Without any outside help, under its own momentum, the rolling snowball grows bigger and rushes forward faster. So it can be with the library profession. When we have set in motion our own critical mass, coalitions with others will come easy. Critical masses have a magnetic force. All of the other information-sector workers will be drawn into the orbit.

The challenges of this era require our leadership to assume the initiative now. Our aims can be met only if the superwomen and the supermen within the ranks of the profession step forward. We need the thoroughness, patience, and tenacity of a Melvil Dewey; the intense scholarship of a Leon Karnovsky; the innovative zeal of a Clara Jones.

Most of all, the awesome mission of library leadership requires that librarians be true to one another. In unity, with all kinds and all types of librarians dedicated to the same set of priorities and the same mobilization plan, librarians can go forward confidently. In the mainstream of decision making, librarians will then prevail.

Pay Equity and the Public Good
Winn Newman

Over the last twenty years, even under past Republican administrations, we've depended on the support of the federal government on civil rights issues. That time has passed. I need not say
that we are living in hard times in terms of where we now stand
with the federal government on civil rights issues. We do not have
much support today. Indeed, when the *Washington State* case
came up for appeal in the Ninth Circuit recently, we met with the
Solicitor General of the United States to discuss the government's
position on the case. We did not urge that the federal government
become involved, on our side, because that was assumed to be an
impossibility with the Reagan administration. What we urged, instead, was that the government not intervene—on the side of the
state! Just before the 1984 election, the White House, not the
Solicitor General, announced that the government would not enter
the case at that time. However, the possibility remains open that
the federal government *will* enter the case at some later date, and
if it does, I think it fair to assume that the government will enter
on the side of Washington State.

We now must recognize that the full weight of the federal
government is against us in all areas of civil rights, and especially
so in this area of wage discrimination. The remarks of Commissioner Clarence Pendleton, the Chair of the Civil Rights Commission, denouncing pay equity as the "looniest idea since looney
tunes" perhaps reflect the extreme of government officials' views.
One wonders whether such a person, who obviously harbors
extremely hostile attitudes towards working women, can properly
head a commission supposedly interested in the rights of all working people, including the rights of working women. That same
commission held hearings on "comparable worth," the outcome

of which was clearly determined in advance. Aligned with the Civil Rights Commission on the wage discrimination issue are the Equal Employment Opportunity Commission, the Department of Labor and the Department of Justice.

All of this put together means we have a rough row to hoe. Increasingly, organizations like ALA will have to play the role once played by government—the protector, defender, and enforcer of the nation's civil rights laws. As such, it is important to have a clear understanding of the legal framework within which this whole issue of wage discrimination arises.

THE ISSUE: SEX-BASED WAGE DISCRIMINATION

We know that where ever a study is done, whatever city does it, there is an average of twenty percent disparity between what librarians are paid and the compensation of male professionals with like training. And we know that these types of disparities are a major culprit in the seemingly intractable wage gap between men and women, captured so eloquently in the "59 percent" slogan.

What doesn't get enough attention, however, is the law—Title VII of the Civil Rights Act of 1964—and how it applies to discriminatory wage practices. ALA's Commission on Pay Equity is one of the few organizations which in its policy statements on pay equity has spelled out its support for the efforts of those library workers who have documented and are now legally challenging discriminatory salary practices. This support for current legal efforts is so important because so many organizations have adopted policies for pay equity which seem not to recognize that we *already* have a law that requires the elimination of discrimination in compensation. Unfortunately, too few people are utilizing that law.

Let me begin by straightening out some terminology, because the terms have been so distorted. One term that ought to be dropped from our lexicon is "comparable worth." Title VII prohibits *discrimination in compensation*. There is no question about that law and what that law does. How it applies is another matter, but certainly the law prohibits *wage discrimination*. And even the most right-wing people—the Phyllis Schlaflys, the Richard Viguerie—agree that discrimination exists. To quote Viguerie, "Certainly there is discrimination against women. I believe discrimination exists. The question is what should be done to eliminate it?"

I place so much stress on this legal point and terminology because, unfortunately, we have allowed our opponents to talk in terms of "comparable worth" and to raise esoteric questions regarding such things as a job's intrinsic worth. This deflects attention from the important legal and social issues underlying the pay equity movement and focuses it instead on nonsensical and inflammatory allegations, similar to those utilized to defeat the ERA. We need to shift this focus and pose the question as follows: Given the fact that the law prohibits discrimination in compensation and that virtually everybody agrees that discrimination against women (and minorities) exists, what are we going to do about that discrimination? We are beyond the point of arguing whether it exists. We are beyond the point of arguing whether it's illegal. The question is how to remedy and end discrimination.

Courts address the issue of sex- and race-based wage discrimination by determining whether, because of sex or race, a particular employer pays employees in traditional "female" jobs or employees in traditional "minority" jobs less than those in traditional "male" jobs (white male jobs) which require similar skills, efforts, and responsibilities. This question of wage discrimination by an individual employer has nothing to do with national wage rates, nothing to do with what other employers pay—it is strictly a question of how a particular employer treats female or minority employees as compared to its white male employees. Viewed in this way, wage discrimination is a much simpler issue—not only simpler but much more easily proved. The issue is not what jobs are intrinsically worth; the issue involves the way a particular employer pays its female and minority employees in comparison with the way that employer pays its white male employees. If in this employer's establishment the white male forklift operator is getting $4 an hour, then women doing work requiring equal skill, effort, and responsibility should not be paid less simply because they are in traditional women's jobs. Similarly, if across the street an employer is paying forklift operators $6 an hour, then women or blacks in traditionally segregated jobs who are doing work of equal skill, effort, and responsibility for that employer should not be getting less because they're in "women's" jobs or "black" jobs.

Proving Sex-Based Wage Discrimination

Once the issue is placed in its proper focus, we need to discuss how one goes about showing that the wages are discriminatory and how to correct the discrimination. The theory of race-based or sex-based wage discrimination is not a new one. Indeed, it is based on the Civil Rights Act of 1964. Courts have held that both sex-based wage discrimination and race-based wage discrimination violate this law. Although not generally known, the earliest wage cases under the Civil Rights Act, dating back to 1968, were race-based wage discrimination cases. In the sex-discrimination area, the earliest successful cases were in the private sector. For example, *IUE* v. *Westinghouse* is one of the leading cases; it dealt with sex discrimination in the electrical industry. *IUE* involved a job evaluation study Westinghouse had done in 1939 for the purpose of standardizing wage rates throughout its plants. Male jobs with the same job evaluation scores as the female jobs were assigned to parallel labor grades, numbered one through five. However, across the board, the pay range for female jobs was fifteen to twenty percent less than that for male jobs with the same point values. The female job with the highest job evaluation score had a lower pay grade than the male job (common labor) with the lowest job evaluation score.

After Title VII became effective, Westinghouse abolished its explicitly separate male and female pay scales and merged the classification lines. However, the women's jobs were placed at the bottom of the unified classification line in labor grades one through five. All of the male jobs were classified in labor grades six or above. This system perpetuated the wage differential first established in 1940, and all men, regardless of the positions they occupied, were paid more than all women. Evidence of these kinds of historical practices is highly probative of present intentional discrimination. Similar evidence is undoubtedly available in many other cases.

EMPLOYER ARGUMENTS

How do employers and the government defend or justify wage discrimination? They generally raise four arguments. First, they argue, we should open the doors to women so they can have greater access to other occupations. But the courts and Congress have rejected the argument that the remedy for wage discrimination is greater access to jobs. Second, as I alluded to earlier, employers argue that a job's true worth cannot be determined, hence it is impossible to measure what jobs should be paid. There is an easy answer to this argument: employers regularly measure job values and set pay rates accordingly. The only problem is they apply different standards to women's jobs and men's jobs, and that is precisely what the law prohibits.

Third, the argument is made that correcting wage discrimination will cost too much. This cost argument is fascinating. In no other area of the law does one openly say, "I'm going to violate the law because I can't afford to comply with the law." This is akin to saying "Social Security is increasing next year, so I won't pay it"; or "the Equal Pay Act has been passed; I'm not going to pay it because I can't afford it"; or "the minimum wage has been increased, I won't pay; I can't afford it." Clearly, cost is no defense of discrimination, and the Supreme Court has so held. Beyond that, however, the cost argument is almost always a makeweight. Fairfax County, for example, has argued that it cannot afford to increase the pay of librarians. Recently, however, the county announced that it has a budget surplus and has proposed a tax

The argument that is most troublesome is the so-called "market" argument. It is a defense which would allow employers to say, "If everybody else is underpaying people, I can underpay them. If everybody else is discriminating, I can discriminate." Again, the argument is generally a makeweight. If we look at how employers determine market rates, we find that they do not make any real attempt to pay what everyone else pays because there is not one standard rate in the market. For example, for certain jobs, wages vary from $3.00 an hour to $5.00 an hour, depending on the employer. There are also different markets for different jobs. The market for a librarian or an academic dean may be a lot different than the market for a typist. In the final analysis, then, the market argument is really a pretense and should be treated as such. In addition, the Supreme Court rejected the market as a defense to the Equal Pay Act in *Corning Glass Works* v. *Brennan* and the same rationale should apply to discriminatory practices under Title VII.

An additional argument raised is that the reason men get higher pay than women is that their work is heavier, dirtier, and/or more dangerous. This argument collapses entirely when analyzed in the context of jobs and industries with a high black concentration. For example, black workers in the paper industry are highly concentrated in the heavy, dirty, physically hazardous jobs. Similar patterns exist in the steel industry and in other industries. The Urban Environment Conference has reported that, as a result of their concentration in these types of jobs, black workers face thirty-seven percent more risk of illness, twenty percent more risk of job-related deaths, and that they are one and one-half percent more likely to be severely disabled from job injuries or illness than white workers. The report, entitled "Reagan, Toxics and Minorities," also concludes that minorities are assigned the dirtiest, most hazardous, and potentially life-threatening jobs in industries characterized by hazardous jobs and unhealthy working conditions. Are black workers paid more because of these "risk factors"? Absolutely not: the black jobs are also the lowest paid in these industries.

This example again reveals the tie between sex-based and race-based wage discrimination. I stress this tie because those of us at the forefront of the women's movement have suffered by allowing wage discrimination to be thought of as solely a women's issue. We need to refocus society's thinking in this regard. We have to say this is a sex and race issue. And in the same way that we do not tolerate open reference to and differential treatment between employees in "black" jobs and "white" jobs, we cannot allow society to continue thinking in terms of "women's" jobs and "men's" jobs which can be treated differently under the law. It is important to show liberals of my vintage that race and sex issues here are basically the same.

SEX-BASED WAGE DISCRIMINATION AND LIBRARIANS

How do librarians fit into this picture? In specifically addressing the wage rates of librarians, we begin with the unquestionable premise that the original structuring of the librarian system was built upon the notion of using cheap, literate labor. This premise is reflected in the attitude, "we can get women cheaper." In 1877, Justin Winsor, a leader in the library profession, publicly stated: "In American libraries, we set a high value on women's work. They soften our atmosphere, they lighten our labor, they're equal to our work, and *for the money they cost* they're infinitely better than equivalent salaries will produce of the opposite sex." Clearly, the "high value" placed on "women's work" was not reflected in extra compensation.

Nothing has changed today—in Fairfax County or elsewhere. Librarians have traditionally been women and, as a result, librarian wage rates have been discriminatorily depressed. The fact that men are now entering the field is not going to change the wage differential which exists between librarians and traditional male professions. The basic wage is still the result of historical segregation; segregation and wage discrimination go hand in glove. This is no different from what the Supreme Court said of school segregation cases thirty years ago—that separating the races denotes inferiority and results in inferior education. Separating the work force by sex also denotes inferiority and results in inferior wages and other conditions of employment.

In Fairfax County, where I suspect employment practices are no different than elsewhere in the country, librarians with master's degrees are being paid less than people with bachelor's degrees in other traditionally male professions. Librarians receive *forty percent less* than other male professionals with master's degrees. A similar kind of disparity exists for other predominantly female professional occupations, such as social workers and mental health therapists. In fact, women in these occupations receive about the same pay as the refuse superintendent who is required only to have a high school education.

Fairfax County attempts, like other employers, to justify the wage disparity by talking about the "market rate" librarians are paid. In the words of the chairman of the board of supervisors, "If you can buy librarians or anything else at a cheaper price you're going to do it." As an aside, when Fairfax County conducted its "market survey" to determine its librarian pay rates, it excluded from the survey the District of Columbia, where the pay rates for librarians are higher. This is a graphic example of how employers can manipulate surveys to juggle market rates.

Just as importantly, the Supreme Court, in interpreting the Equal Pay Act some ten years ago, made clear that unlawful wage discrimination doesn't become legal just because it is cost effective or other employers also discriminate. In *Corning Glass* v. *Brennan* the Court stated:

> The differential between men's and women's wages arose simply because men would not work at the low rate paid women. This reflected a job market in which Corning Glass could pay women less than men for the same work. As a matter of economics it is understandable that the company took advantage of the situation, but its differential nevertheless became illegal once Congress enacted into law the principle of equal pay for equal work.

What the Court was saying is that just because you can get people cheaper because everybody else discriminates, it doesn't make the discrimination legally acceptable under the Equal Pay Act. Nor should it justify discrimination under Title VII.

The final question is how to measure discrimination; how do we determine what portion of the wage gap between women and men is due to wage discrimination as distinguished from other factors. This is not an impossible task; it can be done. In the case of librarians, this is relatively simple because we are dealing with wage rates for entry-level positions (in the sense that they don't require experience in addition to educational training). If we compare these jobs to other entry-level jobs requiring similar educational standards but no prior experience, we begin to get a feel for precisely how much of the disparity comes from discrimination. Then, whether jobs are compared at the entry level, after one year of experience, two years of experience, or five years of experience, we will find a wage disparity. In fact, the disparity increases as we advance to higher steps in the career ladder. The solution is to adjust the entry-level rate and make corresponding adjustments throughout the entire line of progression. Only by elevating the wages of the occupants of the jobs whose wages have been discriminatorily depressed can we correct wage discrimination.

CONCLUSION

There would seem to be no question, since it is conceded that discrimination exists, that law-abiding employers should be willing to look at their wage rates and make voluntary changes. To date, this is not happening. Unfortunately, most employers do not take voluntary action if it is going to cost money. Correcting wage discrimination is going to cost money. It is going to cost because the pay of people in occupations whose wages have been discriminatorily depressed must be increased.

What is needed at this point, then, is litigation strategy. After years and years of attempting to educate people to do the right thing regarding race discrimination, to get them to take voluntary actions, we learned that sometimes the best way to educate is to legislate. And once laws were passed, we learned that the best way to educate is to litigate under those laws.

That is the direction in which we now must head in the wage discrimination area. In the end, I am sure that such actions will make the workplace fairer for us all.

The Library's Role in Supporting the Economic Health of the Nation

Gordon M. Ambach

As we plan coalition building for the future, we need to be aware of the changing nature of both the *workforce* and the *workplace*. Let me briefly note some of these changes.

In the twenty-first century, a relatively smaller workforce, including a proportionately larger component of racial and ethnic minorities, will have to support a relatively larger population of elderly retired people.

The Census Bureau projects that in the period from 1980 to the year 2000, the elderly population, those 65 and over, will grow at a rate of thirty-six percent—the largest percentage growth of any group in the U.S. At the same time, the traditional college-age cohort is projected to *decline* by fifteen percent. As we move into the next century, that smaller college-age group will move into the workforce. The Social Security Administration projects that as the "baby boom" generation begins to retire, the ratio between those in the active labor force and the recipients of Old Age Survivors and Disability Insurance (mostly retired workers) will begin to drop significantly: from 3.2 workers to one recipient in 1983 to 2.0 to one by the year 2035.

At the same time that the demographics of the workforce are changing, the characteristics of the work to be performed are also shifting. Our economy is shifting from a manufacturing base to one based on information and the production of high-technology goods and from labor-intensive to highly automated production. These changes will place additional demands on the skills of workers and managers and require upgrading the workforce.

All indications are that the education level necessary for productive participation in the workforce will become increasingly important in the future. From 1940 to 1980, the proportion of jobs in the U.S. requiring less than a high school education *decreased* from 71.5 percent to 44.6 percent, while the proportion of jobs requiring a college degree *increased* from 7.7 percent to 21.7 percent.

These structural changes will force workers to learn new skills and to adapt to new job demands. All of us are facing the potential of tremendous dislocation and a mismatch between the current knowledge base and future demands. For example, of six blue-collar jobs that have been lost in the steel industry, it is estimated that only *one* will be recovered; in textiles, only *one of thirteen.*

On the other hand, small businesses and entrepreneurship are the most promising areas for the creation of new jobs. Nationwide, small businesses—those with fewer than twenty employees—are responsible for *one-half* of all new jobs. But small businesses are less stable and have less capacity for in-house training. Obviously, then, they can benefit from training assistance provided by educational institutions and libraries.

The changing demographics of the workplace make the training and education of adults a linchpin of human resource development. The baby boomers have already entered the workforce, but the growth rate of the workforce has slowed dramatically. Today's workers will constitute well over ninety percent of the workforce in 1990 and more than seventy-five percent in the year 2000. Retraining skilled workers, professionals, and managers must have a high national priority because the change from an industrial base to an "information society" will continue to create new demands on individuals. In 1950, seventeen percent of our workforce was engaged in information-related work. In 1983, fifty-six percent of the workforce was so employed, and the estimate for 1990 is *sixty-five percent.* According to U.S. Bureau of Labor Statistics forecasts, by 1990 some seventeen to twenty-six million new job opportunities will develop in the United States. An overwhelming number of these jobs will be related to development, production, and servicing in high-technology and information industries.

The movement toward jobs requiring a more sophisticated labor force makes new forms of employee training and retraining imperative. The crucial issues are: who provides that training and who pays for it? The importance of information as a key economic asset forces attention to how we produce, access, and distribute it. These are issues for the nation as a whole, and not just for individual localities, states, or private companies or enterprises.

Just as banking and health care have been decentralized in the United States, so also has education. Schools and colleges are not the only providers of education in our nation now. Computers, telecommunications, and special-purpose programs, from Julia Child to Stanley Kaplan, are readily available. As a result, learning has changed: it is more self-directed and self-managed; it is more readily adaptable to individual schedules; it comes at lower cost and is therefore more and more competitive; and it may lead to credit awarded on the basis of examinations or assessed experience. The emphasis is now on what the learner *knows* rather than on where he or she learned it.

LIBRARY ACTIONS

Libraries have always nourished self-directed study. The potential for expansion of that function is great; the obligation to provide "equity" is even greater. The expanding body of privately funded information resources provided by telecommunications and computers has widened the gap between haves and have-nots. Free public access has meant equity. The challenge to continue providing equity grows daily.

There is a range of initiatives that libraries can take to promote equitable economic development. I suggest four points: adult literacy, pre-employment preparation, job retraining, and research for economic growth. I do not suggest that all libraries initiate activities in each of these areas. Each should use its own strengths to develop programs geared to these ends. Developing a coalition to promote a particular job retraining program or business information project is likely to result in support from coalition partners involved in that special project for other, broader library-service programs. But ALA's strategy should cover all these areas.

ADULT LITERACY

One critical problem our nation faces is the alarming rate of adult illiteracy. While there are no firm statistics, there are millions of Americans unable to read well enough to function in their daily lives. Some of these are persons who never completed school; others are immigrants whose native language is not English.

There is a clear statistical relationship among ethnic minority status, economic disadvantage, and educational underachievement. The disadvantaged part of the population is growing rapidly. Yet we are all going to rely more and more heavily on this population group. It is in society's best interest to fully develop that talent.

Providing all of these groups with literacy skills will enable them to make a greater contribution to our economy and enhance the quality of their lives. It will also help them acquire parenting skills so they can pass the benefits of learning on to future generations and break the cycle of poverty and disadvantage.

Literacy programs are provided in many different settings– by volunteers working as one-to-one tutors, in public schools, colleges and universities, community-based organizations, labor unions, and in business and industry. Each of these providers can be an important part of a coalition for the public good.

Libraries have a significant role to play in eradicating the curable ill of adult illiteracy in America. The success of the California Literacy Campaign, established in 1983 by the California State Library with a $2.5 million commitment of federal LSCA funds, is an excellent example of the strong role public libraries can play in developing community-based literacy projects. This program was so successful that it began receiving state funds in 1985. The campaign takes full advantage of the structure, facilities, materials, and services which libraries can provide to support local literacy projects.

Libraries often have the materials to assist tutors and students; the facilities to provide space for tutor training classes and tutoring sessions; the equipment to assist students requiring computer-based education; convenient hours of operation to accommodate adults who are working; the advantage of having multiple outlets in many small communities; and the firm foundation of information services necessary to promote literacy services and to refer people to programs that best meet their needs.

In Illinois, the state librarian has granted nearly $500,000 to libraries to provide for the development and support of local literacy programs. These funds serve seventeen literacy programs in which local libraries and library systems work with other agencies to establish and support a wide variety of reading programs.

With the aid of over $200,000 in LSCA funds, public libraries in New York State act as local training centers, provide books and other materials for adult learners, and promote volunteer efforts. Many long-established literacy programs, such as that of the Queens Borough Public Library, have waiting lists of prospective students. Library staff recruit, train, and supervise volunteer tutors who teach reading and basic math to functionally illiterate adults. Queens Borough also prepares students to join adult basic education classes by offering pre-ABE math and reading classes in the library.

Basic literacy skills are of fundamental importance not only for entry-level and service jobs but also as the basis for further training and employment advancement. For those reasons, supporting basic adult literacy is a direct service to economic development.

INITIAL JOB PREPARATION—YOUTH SERVICE

Successfully achieving the transition from school to work is an important step toward the goal of becoming a productive citizen and worker. Any strategy to enhance employability—particularly of unemployed, disadvantaged youth—must include three points:

- assuring that each student has a sound basis in basic skills

- providing the basic job skills necessary for initial employment

- developing work habits and a "work ethic" involving both attitudes and knowledge of the work place.

The most essential education in preparation for employment, especially for those who will seek employment after secondary school, is a thorough grounding in the foundation skills of communication and computation. These foundation skills are not only at the core of general education—they are increasingly at the core of occupational education. As our society's jobs turn more toward information and service enterprises, the "job-related skills" are the very same kinds of communication and computation skills that we have always considered to be the heart of general education.

School libraries which share their services and resources with those of other library systems can create effective programs for teaching these foundation skills. They have special roles in helping students to learn the discipline of effective search for and use of information; reinforcing the interdisciplinary character of learning by providing materials that illustrate, for example, that good science can be good reading; and, expanding the student's exposure to materials that go well beyond regularly assigned texts.

Libraries must give special consideration to those students who have traditionally not done well in the elementary and secondary schools or who, by their own decision to drop out, are not even a part of the expanded school standards and reforms currently being implemented.

For the youths, special intervention is necessary; this is not only important for these youths but for the entire nation. Earlier I cited the changing demographics of the work force. I stress the point that our society in the twenty-first century will have to rely to a much greater degree on minority youths who are now economically disadvantaged to carry the economic machinery of the nation. Let me provide some examples of special education and training that is necessary.

The major related federal program now in place is the Job Training Partnership Act (JTPA), the successor to CETA. I note particularly the strengthened emphasis in JTPA on *education and training for employment*, rather than on subsidized employment, as in CETA. This change recognizes that *education* is a key strategy for employment. Forty percent of all JTPA Title II funds are required by legislation to be spent on youth, both in school and out of school. At least ten of the twenty-five fundable activities listed under JTPA are services libraries provide right now.

Funding from JTPA can be pooled with resources available from other federal and state legislation—such as the Vocational Education Act (VEA) and Adult Education Act (AEA)—in order to exert the greatest possible leverage for action. In the first nine months of operation, almost 2,000 young people received basic skills instruction under JTPA in New York State. We expect this figure to grow considerably.

In the 1984 session, the New York State Legislature established a new way for schools to calculate for state aid purposes the attendance of sixteen to twenty year olds in programs leading to equivalency diplomas (GED). This change, together with the appropriation of $5.8 million for adults in equivalency programs, dramatically reduced waiting lists for these much-needed programs. Each year in New York, some 50,000 GED's are awarded, one of every five diplomas. The GED diploma has national credibility. For youth who have fallen severely behind and tend to simply drift away in discouragement, the new "equivalent attendance" program provides an opportunity for success in a changed environment.

JOB RETRAINING

The education and library communities have strong capabilities of joining with business and industry to form retraining programs for skilled workers, professionals, and managers. Some of these dislocated workers have become structurally unemployed in declining industries; others may be subject to changing demands within existing jobs, or may need to keep their knowledge current within a changing discipline. For example, it has been estimated that the "half-life" of a chemist's employment in today's rapidly changing technological environment is *five to six years.* Then chemists must be retrained. No matter how good the initial preparation, continuing education in most fields is essential.

Continued training of the workforce is a major education and economic development challenge. Concentration on this issue will mean the difference between an economic development policy that is successful, and one that fails. Remember, seventy-five percent of the workforce in the year 2000 is already employed now.

Here are some examples of continued training programs in New York State. Employer-specific training provides programs packaged and coordinated to meet targeted training needs identified by employers. The training frequently takes place on-site. It is funded with federal money from the Job Training Partnership Act and Vocational Education Act, supplemented by state appropriations for training dislocated workers. These programs help create new jobs and upgrade many more. The upgrading programs are critical because they result in increased productivity for those directly affected and in "backfilling" of additional new hires.

Our targeted training programs are coordinated through regional economic development centers created in 1983. The providers involved in the programs exemplify the crucial sharing of responsibility between public and private, non-profit and for-profit sectors.

Access to accurate and complete information about available education and training programs is clearly of crucial importance. In New York, educational "brokering services" are available through seven education information centers, all but one located in public libraries and building on their existing capabilities and resources. EIC's provide free, individualized career and educational counseling services in a neutral setting. Initially financed by a foundation grant, our EIC's are now supported by state funding.

The questions of *how* continuing training ought to be provided and *who* ought to pay for it raise major nationwide policy issues. A variety of approaches has been suggested. One is a tuition-assistance program, which some refer to as a "GI Bill for dislocated workers"; a tax-free Individual Training Account, or ITA, which might be established for each individual to draw on for training, is a concept now being debated in Congress. Other concepts include tax credits to companies for investment in education or training of employees; use of unemployment insurance or pension funds for training purposes; and direct grants to providers to offer training programs. Libraries should have a role in all these approaches.

ROLE OF RESEARCH IN ECONOMIC DEVELOPMENT

Research and development are fundamental to strengthening the economy, especially as we shift toward high technology industries. Similarly, as our society rapidly becomes more information-based and information-driven, it is essential for business and industry to locate, acquire, organize, and use information. Here is an area in which libraries provide a vital resource to improve the business climate.

I noted earlier the increased importance of small businesses in the economy. In view of this trend, our educational system must help develop and support entrepreneurs. Dun and Bradstreet statistics show that one-half of new business insolvencies occur in the first five years, and that ninety percent of those failures are due to mismanagement. Education and continuing information services in all areas of management meet crucial needs of small businesses. Entrepreneurs seek out, on their own, the information they need to meet their business and professional objectives in public, university, and corporate libraries and through the networks that link these resources. The information available ranges from specialized business collections, including trade statistics, government specifications, and demographic data, to "how-to" shelves offering books on marketing, inventory, or general management. Through the medium of computer literacy programs, libraries also help small businesses test their need for assistance in using computers.

The information libraries provide is vital not only to research but also to operations and decision making. Every day, business, science, and technology sections of public and university libraries provide technical reports, international trade information, economic data, federal standards and specifications, copies of patents, and a wealth of other information needed for business and industrial purposes.

In New York, our nine reference and research library resource systems (3R's) are linked to each other, joining research, corporate, academic, and public libraries and making it possible for users to secure information and materials from any library in the state. Computer terminals at our state library in Albany make it possible to use more than 2,000 computerized indexes to several million journals and other publications on subjects ranging from multi-bank companies to gas chromatography. Searches which would require weeks of effort by research assistants can be made in minutes at nominal cost.

I have identified certain key aspects of change in our nation's economic structure and employment patterns, and suggested four specific areas of intervention for libraries to support the nation's economic development. First of all, it is necessary to understand the changing workforce and workplace. The next step is to assess the importance of libraries and education services in strengthening workforce skills and capacities. Finally, I have identified the key programs libraries can provide to directly assist the nation's economic growth.

No one institution in this country is responsible for or can provide economic health. Coordinated policies and practical coalitions are essential. In the next decade, fifteen million new workers will enter the workforce. Along with them, the 100 million who are currently employed will require additional training and retraining to meet changing job requirements. Training and retraining are also urgently needed for some 3.5 to 4 million Americans who are now chronically unemployed. Can libraries handle all that? Of course not, but there is a clear role and a challenge to handle part of the task, and the challenge can be met through coalitions.

We often forget how far we have come in this nation. Two hundred years ago, one youth in ten completed high school. Fifty years ago, it was one in three. Now it is about three out of four. That is a remarkable increase in high school completion rates over two centuries. In 1900, five percent of the workforce was involved in work demanding technical skills. Today, the figure is seventy-five percent. This change has occurred in only eighty-five years.

There is still much more that needs to be done. We must build coalitions with business councils and chambers of commerce, and with educational and information-service organizations at the national, state, regional, and local levels. These coalitions need to focus on direct economic development actions. But there is also a need for *indirect* action or service.

Those who analyze business and industrial productivity in the United States have generally concluded that the key to improved quality and productivity is improved motivation, *not* technical skill. It is commitment to quality, to the goals of the enterprise, and to a harmonious work environment that spell success.

The quality of life for individuals and communities is shaped by our personal and social purposes and values. This is true not only in the workplace, but in all other areas of our lives. Our values determine how we live our lives and those values, in turn, reflect our exposure to the treasures and records of our civilization— our art and music and literature—through the resources of our cultural institutions. In that sense, this nation's economic health and culture are inextricably connected to our libraries.

Library Services to Minorities
Mary Hatwood Futrell

As president of National Education Association, the nation's oldest and largest organization of educators, I feel at home with members of the 108-year-old American Library Association, the oldest and largest library organization in the world. The NEA counts nearly 18,000 school librarians among its members. Many of them, I am sure, are also members of the ALA. Our two great organizations share many other links as well. Teachers and librarians have long stood shoulder to shoulder in the battle against illiteracy. We shall continue this common struggle, and I am here to pledge that the relationships we have forged in the past—relationships that have benefitted us both—will continue.

We have made substantial progress toward our goal of a literate America. A recent report by Daniel Boorstin, the Librarian of Congress, tells us that ninety-nine percent of Americans can be classified as literate. However, that's no reason for complacency, there are still twenty-seven million Americans—more than one in ten—who can't read or write well enough to handle simple, daily, necessary communication tasks.

NEA members are committed to meet the goal of full literacy among our population, a goal which demands quality public schools and quality libraries. We are working for this in every way we can. We work for quality schools and libraries in America's smallest communities as well as in the mighty halls of Congress. We strongly believe that a comprehensive library/media program— a program that includes printed and nonprinted resource materials and a certificated librarian/media specialist—should be provided for each and every elementary and secondary school in the United States.

85

Our battle for quality, as we all know, hasn't been easy. In 1984, the Reagan administration proposed budget cuts that would have eliminated important public service funds for libraries. In the areas of public library services, inter-library cooperation, library career research and training, and public library construction, the proposed budget for the 1985 fiscal year was zero dollars. It has always amazed me how, on the one hand, people talk about excellence, and on the other hand, they fail to realize that without resources like well equipped libraries, true excellence becomes more difficult to achieve. I am happy to report that these proposed cuts never went through because Congress stopped them. But that's not the end of this story. Thanks to the hard work of library supporters all across our nation, Congress not only restored the cuts, but actually increased library funding. More than $125 million was voted for library aid! We in NEA regarded this as no small victory.

While the teamwork behind our victory received little credit or recognition, the victory *will* make a difference in the lives of children. The positive impact of this victory will be felt for years to come. I say this because I am confident of it. As a teacher, I appreciate the difference that libraries can and do make for my students.

In school libraries all across America, I have seen the excitement of learning. In a junior high school in Smithville, North Carolina, for instance, I saw a librarian skillfully weave together a project on the local, state, and national elections that was truly inspiring to students. The library also displayed students' art work, examples of structures depicting the evolution of housing. There were also several computers available for students who desired to use them—needless to say it was a very modern, well-equipped library.

In numerous other libraries, in small, medium, and large size communities, librarians' imagination and hard work supplements, supports, and expands the efforts of teachers. My appreciation of each is based on personal experiences; many of these were pleasant— some were not. All helped me to understand and appreciate the value and importance of libraries.

I grew up in Lynchburg, Virginia. As a young girl, I could not go to the largest library—the Jones Library, which was private. I could not even go through the back door. And because transportation was unavailable, the public library located on the other side of town was inaccessible to me. Thus, I relied on the high school library to supplement my classroom learning. While small in comparison to the city's public and private libraries, it opened up the doors of the world for me.

I had another source for acquiring books which was a bit more unorthodox. My mother worked as a day worker (some of you know what that means) and often brought home books which had been discarded by the people for whom she worked. To me the source was not important. Having the books was what I wanted. However, to get back to the point about the books I got from the library, I remember getting so immersed in my library books that I often wouldn't even hear my mother speaking to me. My friends teased me and called me "bookworm."

But the school library was no substitute for a full-fledged library. The selection was very limited. For example, as a young black woman and a child of segregation, it wasn't until I went to college—where I spent hours upon hours in the college library—that I finally had an opportunity to learn about a wide diversity of issues, especially the black experience in this country and my cultural heritage. I learned about assimilation *and* identity in America.

The situation I have described is not a thing of the past. Many communities, and too many schools, lack well-equipped, well-staffed libraries to serve their public. My personal experience convinces me that in the years ahead we must make sure that our library doors swing open to all Americans. Inside those doors must be collections that reflect our nation's true multiethnic and multicultural heritage.

How enriched we would all be if our students—and their parents as well—could walk into an average American library and find the novels of John Oliver Killens, Alice Walker, and Maya Angelou on the shelves. How rewarding it could be if every library carried such marvelous authors as Lydia Cabrera, Ron Arias, Ray Barrio, Tomas Rivera, or Nash Candelaria. How well-informed we could be if our library shelves displayed up-to-date titles on the shame of apartheid and anti-Semitism, the Holocaust and racism, or helped our young people understand their contemporary brothers and sisters who live in the other 169 countries on this planet, to better understand different cultures, geographies, and governments.

Population studies project that by the turn of the century twenty-nine percent of the American nation—almost a third—will consist of four major cultural minority groups: Blacks, Hispanics, Asians, and Pacific Islanders. A quarter century later, more than one out of every three Americans will belong to a minority group. At the same time, our total population will be growing older. In the future—unless other forces intervene—the working, younger population will be contributing heavily to the older, retired, and non-working segment of our society. As I have noted, it is likely that a major part of this workforce will consist of minorities. These minority men and women will then determine the economic health—indeed, the future—of our democratic society.

The challenge is plain: We must be prepared to render all our people—paying special attention to minority populations—the best quality education of which we are capable. Enriched library resources are critical to insuring the quality we need. It is not simply a matter of preparing ourselves for tomorrow's economic and social problems, or the political consequences that flow from those problems. We have a cultural heritage to preserve that cannot be measured in dollars. All people—majority and minority—benefit from an understanding of the cultures that make up our American nation and our world.

It all adds up to a simple bottom line: Libraries are fundamental to educational excellence, fundamental to economic well-being, and fundamental to our democracy. We see this reality clearly. But there are those who would prefer to turn the clock back.

We are all too familiar with those who would decide what's permissible to read, and what isn't. We are all too familiar with the self-appointed guardians of morality. We are all too familiar with so-called "concerned" citizens groups whose idea of morality is banning the word "bed" from the dictionary or harassing teachers who assign *Huckleberry Finn.* Incidentally, my friend Arlene Harris Mitchell—who has studied *Huckleberry Finn* in depth as well as the attitudes of students toward the novel's characterizations and language—points out that this masterpiece of American literature is ninth on the list of the twenty-five most censored books.

I am not going to dwell on the more obvious censorship problems, which we have all been battling for years. The statistics are by now familiar. There have been nearly a thousand attempts, in approximately the last ten years, in at least thirty-four states, to remove more than one hundred different books from libraries and classrooms but I do want to remind you that most of the challenged books are about, or written by, minorities. Censorship is not an isolated phenomenon. It is part of a subtle, but very effective,

attack against the public school system itself. The year 1985 may
see this attack blossom in full. Teachers—and librarians—cannot sit
back idly. For, as certain as the tide of the oceans, the tide of reaction will roll through the doors of your libraries.

Let me tell you about one new weapon in the assault against us:
a notoriously bad piece of federal legislation known as the Hatch
Act. Under this legislation—which went into effect November 15,
1984, teachers find themselves under federal investigation if they
merely assign students to write an essay expressing their own
opinions. Teachers can find themselves under investigation if they
direct a child to a guidance counselor, assign a child to a special
class, test a child for grade level, or provide one-on-one help for a
child with a special need. Under the Hatch Act, any parent who
protests what and how a teacher is teaching can bring a complaint
that could launch a federal investigation—and cost a teacher's
school district all the federal aid that district receives.

How did these incredible regulations come into being? That's
a long story that starts with Phyllis Schlafly and her ultra-right
wing organization, the Eagle Forum. They were able to turn a
fairly innocuous law into a loaded gun against academic freedom.
The Department of Education has the responsibility for administer-
ing the new Hatch Act regulations. As many of you know, the
department has become the nesting ground for right-wing
ideologues.

Right-wing groups have already begun a massive direct-mail
campaign to frighten parents into filing Hatch Act complaints.
Thousands of form letters from parents have poured into local
school offices. The form letters include a parental declaration
that they do not want their sons and daughters participating in
any school session with a guidance counselor, or in any instructional program that touches on values or is designed "for *affective*
training rather than education of the mind."

There seems to me to be a touch of irony in this right-wing
criticism about instructional programs that touch on values. This
criticism comes at a time when more and more commentators are
accusing educators of *not* teaching enough about character building or the historic values of our nation.

Some school administrations are already running scared in the
face of Hatch Act pressure. In Georgia, recently, a school
administration reacted to the pressure by forbidding teachers from
mentioning eight specific topics in any classroom *discussion*:
evolution, abortion as a social issue, communism, religion, witch-

craft, aberrant sex behavior, personal inquiries, and "valuing"—defined as "instructional activities designed to promote decision making and value selection." A high school English teacher has described the paralyzing effect this administrative directive had on her. She was teaching Nathaniel Hawthorne's classic novel, *The Scarlet Letter*, when she suddenly realized she was disobeying the directive. She was teaching her students about witchcraft and religion!

The right wing says the Hatch Act regulations are about parent rights. That's just not true. The Hatch Act regulations don't encourage parents to become true partners in education. What the regulations encourage instead are attacks on academic freedom. The threat is real, and if we do not battle this threat—through legal action, legislative effort, local resistance—then this tide of reaction will drown us.

Some may be able to shrug all this off by saying, "Well, the Hatch Act is a teacher's problem, not a librarian's problem." But I think that the vast majority of librarians and the vast majority of teachers understand fully that an attack on one group's freedom is an attack on the other's as well. No group can morally stand by and allow another's rights to be abridged. Do you remember the words of the German theologian Martin Niemoller? They are words you have heard before, but which nevertheless bear repeating. Niemoller was asked how the terrible tragedies of the thirties and forties came about. He responded:

> In Germany the Nazis first came for the Communists, and I didn't speak up because I wasn't a Communist.
> Then they came for the Jews, and I didn't speak up because I wasn't a Jew.
> Then they came for the trade unionists, and I didn't speak up because I wasn't a trade unionist.
> Then they came for the Catholics, and I didn't speak up because I was a Protestant.
> Then they came for me, and by that time there was no one left to speak for me.

I ask you to work with us even harder than you have in the past to oppose those domestic ayatollahs in our midst. We must penetrate and expose their masquerade. We are not going to run or be scared into the silence of the McCarthy era.

More than two hundred years ago, a great English writer said, "Every society has a right to preserve public peace and order, and therefore has a good right to prohibit the propagation of opinions which have a dangerous tendency." His name was Samuel Johnson.

Mr. Johnson has his place, but forgive me if I prefer John Milton, on whom we all gnashed our teeth and boiled our brains when we were in high school. Almost one hundred forty years before Johnson, Milton wrote in *Areopagitica:* "Whoever knew truth put to the worse, in a free and open encounter?"

The Economic Impact of Libraries: A Dialog in Search of a Coalition

Gerald R. Shields

Economic impact: What does it mean? Does it mean that operating expenditures for academic and university libraries passed the $3 billion mark in 1983; or, that operating expenditures for public school library media centers hit $1.4 billion in 1977 (that's $34.12 per pupil)? Or does economic impact mean that public library expenditures were about $1.5 billion in 1977? Do we add all that up and say that the economic impact of libraries is running somewhere around the $6 billion mark? That seems to have about as much impact in today's federal budget battles as a gnat hitting a windshield going twenty miles an hour.

Those who work in libraries, for libraries, and possibly against libraries know almost instinctively that there must be more to the economic impact of libraries than their expenditures. Gary Purcell, president of Reference and Adult Services Division (RASD) said that "the value of libraries to the public interest of America cannot be measured as a fraction of our Federal budget or gross national product. The value added *far exceeds* the actual expenditure of funds for this service."

Yet, James Nelson, president of the Association of Specialized and Cooperative Library Agencies (ASCLA) was quick to point out that "the direct economic impact [of] libraries represented by ASCLA can be most readily seen in the $400 million-plus spent by state library agencies annually. This money goes to salaries at the state and local level, books and other library materials, construction, telecommunication and other information industry costs, consultant firms, transportation costs and a host of supportive costs required to keep state agencies, public libraries and specialized library services productive." Implied in his statement is the threat that should all of this activity cease there would be a profound effect on the economy in those states.

It is to be expected that the voice coming from the Library and Information Technology Association (LITA) would have a technical ring to it. Yet, here too, the tendency to try and measure effect in terms of dollars spent shows through. "If one selects a very narrow spectrum of the information market place, that of the turnkey vendors who sell hardware/software systems to libraries, the gross revenues for calendar year 1983 was in excess of $64.5 million, a twenty-nine percent increase over 1982. Likewise, if one selects a major bibliographic utility to illustrate the magnitude of such networks, the Online Computer Library Center (a bibliographic utility which serves twenty-nine regional or state library networks, with over 5,000 terminals directly accessing the data base from libraries around the country) reported assets of $71,829,700 and revenues of more than $47 million in 1983, a growth in revenue of over $9.2 million above 1982. . . . The online information selection business has already become a $1.5 billion a year enterprise."

Such figures are certainly impressive, but it is difficult to imagine who else but librarians and online vendors could comprehend the impact of those figures on the economy. Sharon J. Rogers, president of the Association of College and Research Libraries (ACRL), seemed to understand this when she commented on a hypothetical situation.

"Imagine a representative of ALA," she said, "coming before Congress with the raw figures on expenditures. . . . That representative is then faced with the following series of questions: 'You say that college and university libraries (or all libraries) spend a great deal on books, on xerographic equipment, on audiovisual equipment, etc. Well, why not illustrate libraries' importance to those industries by telling us *specifically* what percentage of those markets the library trade represents?' The problem is that not only can we not provide the specific answer, we also cannot provide an estimate and, even more alarming, we cannot even offer a ballpark guess. The numbers simply do not exist."

Ms. Rogers received solid support from Miriam A. Drake, chair of the ALA Committee on Research, in her contention that interpretive reports on economic impact are non-existent. "Searches of the library and economic literatures," said Ms. Drake, "did not produce any studies or statements about the quantitative value of libraries."

There you have it. We seem to be able to generate expenditure statistics but we don't have the interpretive reports to fill in the blanks which might have meaning to those not directly involved in library work. Is that so bad? It is not without reason that the literature harbors no quantitative evaluations of libraries. The American Association of School Librarians (AASL) feels that *its* economic impact is obvious to all:

School libraries will continue to be the foundation for the educational systems which must provide the opportunity for the student to develop those abilities needed to contribute to the economic stability of the local, state, and national level. Well-read, independent library-users, skilled in information retrieval, can successfully become a part of the working populace, thus contributing to a useful, productive, economically sound society and its world.

One would have to be a miscreant to deny these sentiments, but where are the numbers that show the amount of well-read, independent library-users produced and how they measure up as superior members of the working populace?

"We need numbers," asserted ACRL's Sharon Rogers, "to make a case not only before Congress and state legislatures in order to prevent further cuts in direct and indirect funding (e.g. grants, scholarships) for libraries, but we need them to make the best possible case for maintaining or increasing our budget allocation within our . . . institution."

Strangely enough, LITA admits that numbers are good but that they are somewhat shaky. "While . . . statistics provide a measure of growing dollar impact of library and information technology in the U.S. economy, it is critical that the educational mission of libraries in this arena not be forgotten. People must learn how to use these information systems if they are to function in their daily lives."

Gary Purcell of RASD echoed that sentiment from his own perspective:

The economic impact of libraries cannot be measured by the cost of the materials acquired or the salaries paid to the library staff members. The economic impact of libraries in the nation's schools, colleges, and universities is in the knowledge and understanding gained by students and faculty members alike, and by the value-added contribution that they make to society as a result of their access to recorded knowledge, in most cases, available only through their library.

Again, assertions made in terms that exist without any documentation as proof of impact.

Margaret Bush, president of the Association of Library Services to Children (ALSC) seemed to be aware of some significant *numbers* but did not use them when she asserted that "as a society we cannot afford the recent cutting of resources for services to children, whose needs are perhaps more grave and complex than they have ever been in the whole history of the country." This sounds grave. A hypothetical representative in a hypothetical legislature might ask this ALA representative, "Can you give me some figures that demonstrate how the library meets the needs of children? Is this crisis you speak of as being the most grave in our history such that we will need some legislation on the level of child-labor laws?"

Charles W. Robinson, president of the Public Library Association (PLA), acknowledged that there is rising interest in numbers such as the gross national product and other economic indicators as a means of justifying library expenditures, but he is pessimistic that the benefit of libraries is feasible in monetary terms. But, he is not worried:

"Nevertheless," he said, "the contribution to economic health is there, and its existence is generally recognized and accepted, or libraries of all types would have ceased to exist long ago, especially public libraries, whose competition for the tax dollar is repeated on an annual basis." Again, we are comforted by authoritative reassurance of the practicality of libraries. Yet we may feel a bit more comfortable if President Robinson told us where we could find documentation on the generally recognized contribution of libraries to economic health, and *who* are those people who accept our contribution as worthy. There were several libraries around the nation this past year who were faced with proposals in the local budget that they be closed because they were an economic burden.

The most elevated example of optimism—rather than numbers—is exemplified in the statement made by Joan Atkinson, president-elect of the Young Adult Services Division. She contends that open access to information, without direct charge to youth, "... reinforces in a practical way the values contained in the Declaration of Independence, the Constitution and the Bill of Rights. It also encourages economic growth."

Lawrence J. White, a conservative economist at New York University, recognized this reluctance of librarians to quantitatively measure what they do in their service patterns. In his 1983 monograph *The Public Library in the 1980's*, he says that librarians

> ... have largely avoided focusing on usage and the *output* measures against which achievements might be measured. Instead, they have traditionally tended to focus on the needs of the community for more information, more reading material, less illiteracy, and such; on broad, vague statements of the goals and aspirations of the library with respect to those needs; and on the *inputs* (personnel, books and other materials in stock or acquired, on monetary expenditures on these inputs) 'necessary' to meet these needs.

What Dr. White may not understand is that librarians are often faced with the frustration of dealing with data that are confidential in relation to the client's ultimate purposes. Annalee M. Bundy, writing for the Resources and Technical Services (RTSD) ad hoc Task Force on the Economic Impact of Libraries, expressed that feeling at the conclusion of her report. "Throughout this report, it is noted that 'research can be done' or 'data can be gathered.' This is true, but in libraries it is not customary to ask a user what the result might be for the information requested. . . . Much of this information will have to be gathered as a primary source."

On that encouraging note, it is time to take a peek at what went on at the Library of Congress Network Advisory Committee (NAC) meeting in Washington, D.C. in November 1984. The aim of the session was to seek a working definition of the information economy and explain how libraries fit into and are affected by it. Sherman Robinson, economist from the University of California at Berkeley, discussed the use of input-output analysis that has been used in studies by Fritz Machlup and Marc Porat. Robinson interpreted their data to mean that information is an important component of many economic activities and indicated the importance of libraries and information utilities to the economy. He emphasized that libraries and databases should be viewed as capital goods that yield a flow of information services. This would mean that acquisitions in a library should be treated as a capital investment rather than an operating expense. Robinson found the studies limited, however, and he stated that more fine-grained data are necessary for examining the links between libraries and the economy.

At the same session, Michael Turillo, a partner in Peat, Marwick, Mitchell & Co., argued that business and strategic planning techniques can and should be applied to libraries and information services. He suggested that concentration on quality-of-life issues is less important than identifying critical elements related to needs and issues; that partnerships were generally superior to working individually; and that libraries should be looking at cooperative ventures and alliances.

This, then, is the basis for dialog. On the one hand are those librarians concerned with the quality-of-life issues who are suspicious of or fear the outcome of efforts to transpose library services into production charts hanging behind a director's desk. And there are a growing number of librarians who recognize that, as the information age and its "knowledge industry" develops, the library as a resource has to be able to measure its impact if it is to survive in a form that will have a chance to make an impact, not only on the economics of life but on its eventual quality as well. It is possible for such a dialog to proceed if the words of Bernard Berelson can somehow be recalled from the past: "The library's problem is a problem of the optimum allocation of resources. . . . Since it can't be all things to all men, it must decide what things it will be and to whom."

ALA has the forum to provide the widest possible spectrum of interest and concern representing a variety of services and collection development targets. Instead of each faction going its own way, the first coalition should be amongst the units of ALA. Sharon Rogers recognized this in her recommendations for action:

> First, we can at least begin the process of encouraging libraries to routinize their terminology and budget categories.
>
> Second, we can explore whether education research institutes affiliated with major universities would be interested in undertaking this project. . . .
>
> Third, we can explore whether a marketing company (or a collaboration of companies, or a collaboration with a research institution) can examine libraries' expenditures in order to break them down into credible economic categories.
>
> Finally, some private companies selling to educational institutions and to publishers undertake their own periodic research and marketing studies. They do not, however, include at this time the sort of indices that we need to make our case . . . a request from ALA to slightly adapt their categories may not increase their expense to the firm.

Formulating coalitions requires dialog, then compromise, and finally coordination of purpose. ALA is offering this opportunity to its members to improve their ability to report their impact upon the society they serve in a practical way. Since the majority of library and information-service agencies are not-for-profit institutions drawing their support from the public sector, economics seems to be the most desirable place to begin such accountability.

One final admonition as you undertake such an adventure. Remember that, to be effective, these coalitions are going to have to represent the consumers of library services as well as the practitioners of information access and delivery. Joanne C. Wisener, president of the American Library Trustee Association (ALTA), has given us the clue as to where such a coalition already exists. "Trustees are perhaps the strongest advocates within the political process at local, state, and federal levels. Singly, the impact is not successful, but the combination of many involved lay-spokesmen attracts attention from funding agencies."

BIBLIOGRAPHY

American Association of School Librarians: *A Statement*, February 8, 1985.

Atkinson, Joan, Young Adult Services Division: *Contribution to the Economic Health of the Nation*, 1984.

Berelson, Bernard, *The Library's Public* (New York: Columbia University, 1949), p. 134.

Bundy, Annalee M., Resources and Technical Services Division: Ad Hoc Task Force Report: *Forging Coalitions—Economic Impact of Libraries*, 1984.

Bush, Margaret, Association for Library Service to Children: *Statement on the Contribution of Library Services to Children to the Economic Health of the Nation*, 1985.

Drake, Miriam A., ALA Committee on Research: *The Value of Libraries to the Economy*, 1985.

Library and Information Technology Association: *LITA's Interests as They Contribute to the Economic Health of the Nation*, 1985.

Library of Congress *Information Bulletin* 44(5) (February 4, 1985), pp. 21-23.

Nelson, James A., Association of Specialized and Cooperative Library Agencies: *Statement on Economic Impact*, 1985.

Purcell, Gary R., Reference and Adult Services: *Concerning the Economic and Social Impact of Libraries*, 1985.

Robinson, Charles W., Public Library Association: *Public Libraries and the Economic Health of the Nation*, 1984.

Rogers, Sharon J., Association of College and Research Libraries: *Task Force Statement*, October 16, 1984.

Strong, Gary E., Library Administration and Management Association: *Contribution to the Economic Health of the Nation*, 1984–85.

White, Lawrence J., *The Public Library in the 1980s* (Lexington, Mass: Lexington Books, 1983), p. 8.

Wisener, Joanne, American Library Trustee Association: *A Statement of ALTA's Contribution to the Economic Health of the Nation*, 1985.

PART THREE
Coalitions and Libraries

Serving the Public Good: Coalitions for Free Library Services

William Eshelman

The sense of urgency that underlies E. J. Josey's choice of "Forging Coalitions for the Public Good" as the topic for the ALA presidential program is simply that time may be running out . . . as George Orwell envisioned. Whether Orwell chose the year 1984 by whim or foresight, the creative imagination—once again—is mightier than factual information. The reelection of Big Brother as president of the United States in that year has created a need for coalitions of great power and persuasiveness if humanitarian values are to be restored to this nation and sustained.

Unlike medical doctors and lawyers, the nurturing professions— school teachers, social workers, and librarians—devote the major part of their professional lives to *pro bono publico* activities. The two high-prestige, fee-based professions may occasionally perform services for the needy at no fee (out of compassion or guilt), but the three "semi-professions" are duty-bound to serve any and all persons as a major responsibility of their calling.

All libraries are civilizing agencies in society. In the continuing struggle to establish and maintain democratic values, free public libraries are essential for providing information and knowledge, enhancing individual growth, easing the transition from youth to maturity, and setting people on the road to wisdom. Our society has faith in reading as a Good Thing that leads to desirable ends, and it believes reading has the power to alter people for the better.

In a democratic society, the free public library also has a civic aim. It offers citizens the means by which they may become informed and intelligent citizens. Thomas Jefferson believed that the establishment of a small circulating library in every county would be of great value in creating a well-informed citizenry. Where the people have the responsibility for electing public officials, and in our era the additional one of voting on weighty referenda, it becomes imperative that they vote from knowledge, not ignorance.

In implementing the civic aim of the free public library, librarians have the duty to provide as many points of view as possible on current issues. It is not for the library to tell people how to vote, or what opinions to hold on current issues; rather it is up to them to provide a range of views on these issues so that people may make up their own minds about where they stand on the issues.[1]

Of course, public libraries have other, less solemn, goals—meeting practical, utilitarian needs; supplementing school libraries; and providing recreational reading, among others. Academic, school, and special libraries have their individual emphases. But in the most general sense, libraries exist to facilitate communication—between persons of the present and those of the past, between persons in the present, or between those in the present and some future person.

These lofty aims, we have found through bitter experience, are very difficult to defend in a budget meeting. Boards of trustees, academic administrators, school boards, or any other authority that oversees libraries, are simply disbelieving of our altruism. We have not done a good job in explaining the library's vital role, and are constantly assumed to be engaged in empire-building.

That is one reason we need coalitions. A coalition is a temporary alliance of persons, institutions, or groups for joint action. We already have networks, Friends of the Library groups, cooperatives, and other means of increasing influence or power by the force of numbers. Coalitions are viewed not as an alliance of discrete entities, but as a joining together of large, usually national, groups. The sheer size of the federal government, its intricacies and complexities, the bureaucratic sand in its gears—all require more power to effect even a small change. Libraries certainly can no longer "go it alone."

We are not really neophytes in this area, of course. Think of the altruism underlying interlibrary loan (at least in the early days!). Think of the pacts between the libraries of Duke University and the University of North Carolina, or between Stanford and the University of California at Berkeley. These are linkages between private and public institutions—*pro bono publico*. One could go on: the Farmington Plan; the New England Deposit Library; the Center for Research Libraries; NYSILL; RLG; and more. But when we venture outside the library community, we have often asked for help by casting about rather than carefully developing a proposal of what we can do for the other parties.

An example is Eric Moon's visit to Ralph Nader during a time when Moon was planning his ALA presidential year. Mr. Nader listened to various proposals for cooperation and then asked if the ALA could help his organization get libraries to acquire and display his publications. He, too, considered this to be *pro bono publico*. The request was made, but even Moon's prestige as president was not enough to get ALA to respond to Nader's *quid pro quo*.

But let us move to a success story. The Friends of the Detroit Public Library, in a desperate drive to "Keep the Doors Open," scoured the city to identify groups that would join with them in a coalition to help keep DPL afloat—at least for one more year. As one of the cities hardest hit by unemployment (resulting primarily from the incompetence of the scions of the automobile industry there), the DPL had been struggling to preserve even its basic services. The library was designated as a statewide, not just a city, resource, and for a time received additional state funding. But it became clear that the only lasting solution was an increase in the tax rate. Thanks to the hard work of the coalition, the hard-pressed citizens of Detroit voted to tax themselves an additional one mill to support their public library. This amounts to about $5 million more each year.[2]

Some of the credit for the successful campaign must be attributed to good will of the Information & Referral Service, which is an everlasting tribute to the vision of Clara Jones. The linkages forged in the development of that community service will bind the Detroit community to its library for years to come.

A second example is the Wingspread Forum (and its sequel at Wye Plantation) sponsored by the Association of American Universities, the American Council of Learned Societies, and the Council on Library Resources. Among the decisions reached at these meetings was to establish a continuing forum to address the needs of the system of scholarly communication, and CLR pledged to advance this aim.

Two quotations from the reports of the meetings are worth pondering. "To fulfill [scholarly] expectations, it is useful (and probably essential) to think not in terms of individual libraries but rather of 'The Library,' the aggregation of all research libraries, as a key component of the scholarly world."[3] And second, "The new agenda of information service will be superimposed on long-established and still essential archival responsibilities. Libraries (and librarians) will necessarily be full participants in both teaching and research. The changes will affect university and library organization and management, staff composition, costs and funding, service characteristics, external relationships, and the ways scholars work and teachers teach. It is certain only that little we know now of libraries will be left untouched."[4] These reports are the result of a coalition, if you will, although a very select one.

The two examples have one element in common: The role of the library has been redefined. Public libraries have been slow to develop information and referral services, yet the benefits of maintaining this activity may well be more important than the good it does for the community—*pro bono publico*. The linkages formed while maintaining information and referral have resulted in a ready-made coalition that can be called on in times of need, not just to strengthen the library's call for public funding, but also when the library is under attack by bigots of whatever stripe. Academic libraries, if the concept of "The Library" envisioned by the Wingspread Forum is to come to fruition, will also need redefinition. For example, a small college library might well have a rare book or unique manuscript that requires preservation. This would no longer be regarded as a decision to be made locally, but as a requirement in the national—indeed global—interest.

Enlightened self-interest is not the only motivation for building coalitions. In the 1980s, they are essential, for we are in an unprecedented battle against a very powerful group of White House advisors. The Reagan administration has been anti-library on many fronts. It illegally removed members of the National Commission on Libraries and Information Science, intending to replace them with persons sympathetic to White House revisions of a wide range of traditional policies. Among these revisions are: 1) restricting the publication and dissemination of government documents; 2) allowing private entrepreneurs to publish and profit from the sale of information gathered, analyzed, and written at public expense; 3) the downgrading of the qualifications for federal librarians by the Office of Personnel Management; 4) contracting with private firms to provide library service for governmental units, rather than staffing the unit. NCLIS, as now constituted, even supported the White House move to withdraw from UNESCO, in direct contradiction to an ALA resolution.

The *ALA Washington Newsletter* has been tracing the attack on the provision of government information in an appendix, the fourth installment of which covers through June 1984. The head-note to this chronology states:

> What was first seen as an emerging trend in April 1981 when the ALA Washington Office first started this chronology, has by June 1984 become a continuing pattern of the federal government to restrict government publications and information dissemination activities. A policy has emerged which is less than sympathetic to the principles of freedom of access to information as librarians advocate them.

The newsletter cites these implications of the events of the early eighties:

> Contractual arrangements with commercial firms to disseminate information collected at taxpayer expense, increased user charges for government information, the trend toward having increasing amounts of government information available in electronic format only and eliminating the printed version.[5]

The ALA Council has passed a resolution reaffirming that open government is vital to a democracy.

In December 1983 the Joint Committee on Printing received an objection from the Director of the Office of Management and Budget (OMB) to the proposed regulations calling for the Government Printing Office (GPO) to continue distributing all government publications.[6] In April 1984 the Justice Department argued that the regulations were "statutorily and constitutionally impermissible."[7]

In May 1982 the GPO, as directed by OMB, destroyed $11 million worth of government publications that were not selling more than fifty copies a year on earning more than $1,000 a year in sales.[8] In line with this policy, the GPO refused to print forty-four publications requested by the National Bureau of Standards because the predicted sales would be too low.[9] The GPO earlier ceased publication and free distribution of its *Selected U.S. Government Publications*, a monthly list. GPO suggested that readers subscribe to the *Monthly Catalog*—at $90 a year. In line with the mindset of the OMB, the annual subscription to the *Federal Register* rose from $75 to $300, and the *Congressional Record* increased in price from $75 to $208.[10]

By January 1984 the OMB reported that it had eliminated 3,287 publications and consolidated 561; this is one-fourth of the total government inventory. Meanwhile the OMB is continuing its attack on the remaining 9,000 publications, with a view to eliminating as many as possible, and for those it allows to continue it urges reducing the volume, frequency of issues, use of color, and other factors it deems too costly.[11]

In February 1984 the administration proposed, for the third year in a row, the elimination of library grant programs.[12] So far, the Congress has continued to fund these programs, but a coalition to keep the legislators informed could help insure continued funding.

The present administration issued in July of 1981 its Form 4193, which binds government employees to submit all writings, including fiction, for prior censorship review—even after they have left government service. On March 11, 1983 the president signed a directive to broaden the pre-publication review requirement and added the use of polygraph testing in an effort to halt disclosures. Public outcry, part of which was a resolution from ALA, forced the president to rescind this directive eleven months later.[13] A General Accounting Office study completed in July 1984, however, found that at least 120,000 government employees had already signed Form 4193, not including CIA or National Security Agency (NSA) employees. In addition, the study found that almost five million government employees, in twelve different agencies, were subject to pre-publication review requirements during the time of their employment.[14]

Representative Jack Brooks (D-TX) drafted legislation that would outlaw virtually all existing censorship requirements except for the CIA and the NSA. It holds that requiring employees to sign pre-publication review agreements is an "unwarranted infringement of open debate on matters of national importance" and was "readily subject to intentional manipulation and abuse for partisan political purposes."[15] The ALA Code of Professional Ethics states:

> In a political system grounded in an informed citizenry, librarians are members of a profession explicitly committed to intellectual freedom and the freedom of access to information. We have a special obligation to ensure the free flow of information and ideas to present and future generations.

The present administration is working hard to gut the Freedom of Information Act. By regulation, declassification of documents is no longer automatic—a reversal of a thirty-year policy—and the National Archives, which has the authority to review classification decisions, has been precluded from doing so. Executive Order 12356 substantially increased the amount of information that can be classified. The Senate passed S. 774, which increases the confidentiality of certain law enforcement, private business, and sensitive personal records. This regulation adds processing fees to existing search and copying charges.[16] We need a strong coalition now to fight these kinds of measures.

A topic of growing concern is equal pay for "comparable worth." President E. J. Josey has established a Commission on Pay Equity, and the ALA is a member of a coalition, the National Committee on Pay Equity. In the forefront of the movement for comparable pay is another coalition member, the American Federation of State, County, and Municipal Employees, which has 400,000 women among its million members (including a goodly number of librarians). Perhaps the most important ruling so far was in the state of Washington. Judge Jack Tanner decided that Title 7 of the Civil Rights Act of 1964 "was designed to bar not only overt employment discrimination but also practices that are fair in form but discriminatory in operation." Assistant Attorney General for Civil Rights William Bradford Reynolds is spearheading the attack on the principle of comparable worth.[17]

That a person charged with defending civil rights should be thus betraying his role is typical of the present administration. Key appointments in many top jobs in the cabinet and the executive branch were made with the understanding that the persons would strive to reverse the direction mandated by Congress or by prior administrations, undermine the goals of the agencies, and even force long-time career civil servants to resign or retire.

Coalitions are essential for the 1980s because if you lack clout, you're out. More seriously, coalitions are needed because the Reagan administration is opposed to public services in general and libraries in particular.

Item: The National Archives can no longer loan microfilms.[18]

Item: Government documents refused publication by GPO are available only from the National Technical Information Service, which charges two to three times as much for them.[19]

Item: In 1983, private sector firms took over the operation of the libraries for the Department of Energy and the Department of Housing and Urban Development.[20] (Do you think these will be staffed and maintained at the proper level, given the margin of profit?)

Item: The Director of OMB says information is not a free good.

Coalitions for the public good may be the way to reverse these trends. We'll never know unless we try. Shall we overcome?

REFERENCES

1. Curley, Arthur, and Dorothy Broderick, *Carter and Bonk's Building Library Collections* (Metuchen, N.J.: Scarecrow Press, 1985).
2. Berry, John, "Remember Detroit!" editorial, *Library Journal* 109 (September 1, 1984), p. 1575.
3. Haas, Warren J., "Forum I: Toward the 21st Century," *Two Reports on Research Libraries* (Washington, D.C.: Council on Library Resources, 1983), pp. 13-14.
4. Ibid., "Forum II: National and Regional Aspects of Collecting and Preserving Library Materials," p. 48.
5. ALA Washington Office, "Less Access to Less Information By and About the U.S. Government, IV," *ALA Washington Newsletter* (Appendix), p.1.
6. Loc. cit.
7. Ibid., p. 5.
8. ALA Washington Office, II, p. 2.
9. Ibid., p. 3.
10. Ibid., p. 1.
11. ALA Washington Office, IV, p. 2.
12. Ibid., p. 3.
13. ALA Washington Office, III, p. 2.
14. Burnham, David, "Hear No Evil, Speak No Evil, Publish No Evil," *The New York Times* (August 16, 1984), p. B14.
15. Loc. cit.
16. ALA Washington Office, IV, p. 2.
17. Goodman, Walter, "Equal Pay for 'Comparable Worth' Growing as Job-Discrimination Issue," *The New York Times* (September 4, 1984), p. B9.
18. ALA Washington Office, I, p. 4.
19. Loc. cit., II, p. 3.
20. Loc. cit., III, p. 3.

The Effective Coalition*
Joan C. Durrance

In the beginning were the companies
And the companies begat the trade associations
The Pharmaceutical Manufacturers Association
And the American Iron and Steel Institute
And The National Association of Realtors.
And the trade associations and companies begat
The super-associations—The U.S. Chamber of Commerce
And The National Association of Manufacturers
And The Business Roundtable.

And all of these begat the coalitions—
The Clean Air Working Group
And The Longshore Action Committee
And The Ad Hoc Estate Tax Group
And The National Coalitions of Telephone Users and Providers.

Such is the genealogy of the business lobbying community.[1]

The tongue-in-cheek genealogy above shows that the business community knows very well that, on important issues, combined voices are more effective than single voices. Building coalitions to influence decisions in the public policy arena is not a new idea. But coalition formation has increased markedly in the past few years. Since the late seventies, coalitions have formed around "virtually every issue that comes along."[2] According to a recent

*This article draws heavily from the author's book on organized citizen participation, *Armed for Action: Library Response to Citizen Information Needs* (New York: Neal-Schuman Publishers), 1984.

survey, based on a national sample of Washington, D.C.-based corporations, ninety percent of trade associations, unions, and public interest groups regularly enter into coalitions.[3]

There are several reasons why coalitions form so frequently in the eighties. Sociologists have pointed out that the decline of mediating institutions in society "has led to an erosion in the traditional source of consensus making."[4] During the past decade, traditional mediating institutions such as political parties have been superseded by special interest groups. In addition, congressional reforms of the late sixties and early seventies have changed the way Congress operates.[5] The seniority system, long a tradition, has lost its power in the congressional process, and decision making has become more diffuse. These factors have led to the rise of special-interest lobbies: the farm lobby, the transportation lobby, the military, environmental interests, etc.

During this same period, numerous business, professional, and public interest organizations moved their headquarters to the Washington, D.C. area to facilitate lobbying of congressmen and the federal government bureaucracy. Coalitions are the creatures of this activity. Today, more than a third of all corporations, professional organizations, and special-interest groups are either headquartered or have offices in the Washington, D.C. area, providing them with the ideal opportunity to form coalitions with like-minded groups.

Coalitions are effective voices for a variety of interests, but most share certain characteristics, each of which provides an insight into what makes them work. The major elements of an effective coalition are discussed below.

INVOLVEMENT BY MORE THAN TWO GROUPS, OFTEN WITH GRASSROOTS COMPONENTS

The motivation behind the development of most coalitions is that the joint voices of many actors is far more effective in exerting political influence than the single voice. As the *Sierra Club Bulletin* reminded its readers:

> a politician can discount the complaints of a health [group], for example, about the health hazard posed by air pollution. However, when labor organizations, neighborhood councils, senior citizen groups, and medical associations add their voices to those of the health group, the politician can no longer afford to ignore them.[6]

Coalitions formed by trade associations excel at getting grass-roots support of business and industry. For example, the U.S. Chamber of Commerce is composed of 4000 local chamber groups and 96,000 business firms. At various times in recent years, it has held memberships in over eighty different coalitions and "issue strategy groups."[7]

Citizen groups have formed coalitions of multiple organizations involved with a number of issues in an effort to balance the influence of the well-organized corporate community. The difficulty of coalition building has most often been in unifying disparate groups and in their ability to exercise enough influence on their grassroots components. The widely publicized confrontation over the Clean Air Act in the mid-1970s is an early example of the recent emergence of coalitions. A lobbyist for tough emission control standards reportedly mused that although there are more than 200 million proponents of clean air, the challenge he faced was how to mobilize them. The most effective way of mobilizing the grassroots is through the organizations to which they belong. However, joining together in a coalition requires a common cause *and* a mechanism through which members can get out a common message.

Public interest groups often lack the motivating power to get their grassroots growing. *Congressional Quarterly* reports that the corporate special interests are often far more effective, although some of their methods may be suspect. For example, when the Reagan administration's tax cuts were enacted, Congress was under enormous pressure from taxpayers. Much of this pressure "did not spring spontaneously from the soil of popular opinion."[8] Rather, the deluge of letters was orchestrated by special interest activity. *CQ* reports that a management firm sponsored a contest with a prize consisting of an evening's elaborate entertainment. In order to be eligible, contestants had to write a letter to their congressional representative urging passage of the president's economic plan, with a carbon to the management company. "The more letters the better. Use different stationery—change the words—and mail one every few days."[9]

Nearly every trade association or public interest group of any stature has developed its own 'grassroots' network to assure that what its Washington lobbyists say is reinforced by an outpouring from "back home."[10]

COLLECTIVE ACTIVITY OR COORDINATION

Ornstein and Elder did an analysis of the coalition behavior which developed around the amended Clean Air Act.[11] Those who sought a strong Clean Air Act formed a coalition in September of 1973. The National Clean Air Coalition was initially made up of the Urban Environmental Conference, "an urban problems study group"; the Sierra Club (180,000 members); the League of Women Voters (140,000 members); the United Steel Workers; and the American Public Health Association. By November of that year, they were joined by Ralph Nader's Public Interest Research Groups; the National Wildlife Federation; Friends of the Earth (20,000-25,000 members); Environmental Action (15,000 members); Common Cause (250,000 members); the National Audubon Society (375,000 members); and the Oil, Chemical and Atomic Workers (177,000 members).[12]

The coalition kept its members informed through their newsletters and magazines, and through group action calls. In addition, it formed a grassroots network consisting of a core of 150 active environmentalists who were to call a dozen fellow activists when action needed to be taken.

An alliance of labor and business formed in opposition to strong auto pollution standards. That coalition consisted of General Motors, Ford, Chrysler, the Motor Vehicle Manufacturers Association (MVMA), the National Automobile Dealers Association (NADA), the Automobile Service Industry Association, and the United Auto Workers (UAW). Ornstein and Elder point out that the automobile companies which led the fight against the Clean Air Act were not well organized at first, but quickly responded to the circumstances.

Congress was deadlocked on the clean air issue from 1975 until 1977, when it finally passed the amended Clean Air Act. Lobbying on both sides during that period was intense. Paul G. Rogers, House Floor Manager, called it "the heaviest lobbying I've seen in twenty-three years in Congress."[13]

Since the clean air legislation, coalitions have been at work on most major policy issues at the national, state, and local levels. The Citizen Group Information Study found that over half of the citizen groups in Toledo, Ohio are involved in at least one coalition. Block clubs and neighborhood groups have joined to form community coalitions, thus increasing their strength and influence.[14]

Coalitions parallel and extend the activities of their individual members. They monitor government activity and apply direct pressure on legislators and other decision makers, they galvanize grassroots actions around proposed legislation or other public policy decisions, placing a high priority on molding public opinion through the media. They disseminate information about the issue of concern, and they engage in litigation.

The effectiveness of coalitions is due in large measure to the nature of their collective activities. Since they are likely to engage in several different activities at the same time, they must carefully coordinate their staff to make sure that their educating/informing message gets out.

JOINT USE OF RESOURCES

In order to influence public policy decisions, coalitions must not only possess resources, they must also be able to utilize them. To mobilize their members, they must obtain sufficient operating funds and gain access both to decision makers and to public opinion. Shared resources through coalitions make it possible for voices which might otherwise have remained silent to be heard in the public policy arena; they increase the effectiveness of many splintered groups by uniting their voices.

On any public policy issue a minimal resource base is required. A resource floor can be described as the ability to gain sufficient power to be heard. How much is enough? Very simply, in a parade of squeaky wheels, the group's squeak must be audible. Since government in a democracy responds to pressure, this means competing with others to get one's ideas heard. "Power . . . refers to the *possession of resources* (such as money, physical strength, and personal persuasiveness) and the ability *to use* these resources."[15]

In the late 1970s, a group of activists concerned with environmental issues joined with another group concerned with urban issues to form the City Care Conference. Prior to that time, these groups had seen no common areas in which to work. By increasing communication, these groups have shared their resources and developed coalitions to address issues of common interest, including employment, housing, parks, air quality, toxic substances, mass transit, the environment, and the nuclear freeze.[16]

We most commonly think of resources as money and numbers of people, but a valuable resource in getting a group's message across may be the prestige of certain individuals. Coalitions may take out full-page ads paid for by member groups, briefly outlining their position and featuring the names of prominent supporters. The National Mobilization for Survival, a group opposing nuclear escalation, has effectively used such ads, featuring the names of prominent Americans such as Bella Abzug, Arthur Ashe, Ed Asner, Leonard Bernstein, Julian Bond, Dianne Feinstein, Jules Feiffer, Jane Fonda, Linus Pauling, Benjamin Spock, Joanne Woodward, and Andrew Young.

The corporate community is well-structured for effectively using corporate resources to put pressure where it will have the most impact, often applying it from a number of places at the same time. One of its strategies, for instance, is to orchestrate grassroots support for issues of importance to them through employee letter-writing campaigns. The multiple resources used by corporate lobbyists is best understood by looking at some of the trade associations and coalition memberships held by General Motors.[17]

- American Bus Association

- American Public Transit Association

- American Road and Transportation Builders Association

- The Business Roundtable

- Clean Air Working Group

- Committee of Railroad Shippers

- Committee of Truck Shippers

- Highway Users Federation for Safety and Mobility

- Motor Vehicle Manufacturers Association

- National Association of Manufacturers

- National Defense Transportation Association

- Railway Progress Institute

- Transportation Association of America

- U.S. Chamber of Commerce

Trade associations do an excellent job of mobilizing the resources of their members. The Motor Vehicle Manufacturers Association (MVMA) represents General Motors and eleven other automobile, bus, and truck manufacturers. MVMA has a staff of 125, which compiles statistics, conducts research, and engages in legislative monitoring at the federal level and in various state capitals. The association has five divisions, each with particular lobbying functions: communications, government affairs, law, motor truck manufacturers, and technical affairs. There are thousands of trade associations which, when they lobby, speak for "the industry." These organizations provide information for their members and for the coalitions which they form. Trade associations also are responsible for a good deal of grassroots lobbying by employers or constituents. Trade associations often form federated organizations or "super-associations," like the Chamber of Commerce. The Chamber of Commerce

> determines and makes known to the government the recommendations of the business community on national issues and problems affecting the economy and the future of the country. [It] informs, trains, equips and encourages members to participate in policy-making decisions at federal, state, and local levels and in legislative and political action at the national level.[18]

It engages in a variety of activities, such as sponsoring a weekly television program, lobbying, and publishing special reports, studies, and research papers.

Another super-association, the Business Roundtable, counts among its members such firms as General Motors, AT&T, U.S. Steel, Standard Oil of Indiana, and Sears. It prefers to use its own members, "the presidents and board chairmen of corporations," instead of lobbyists because of this elite group's ability to reach members of Congress with relative ease.[19] These associations are called on frequently when congressional members discuss policy issues which affect business.

INFLUENCING OPINION

An effective coalition seeks to have its message heard. This may mean reaching a fairly specific audience or it may mean influencing public opinion and ultimately the appropriate decision makers. Coalitions may prepare papers, reports, pamphlets, information sheets, or even books explaining their viewpoints. *Nuclear War: What's In It for You*, a book which was widely distributed in 1982, was prepared by Ground Zero as an educational tool.

Historian Barbara Tuchman, in an article in *The New York Times Magazine*, praised the role that such citizen groups have played in "the remarkable change in this country from recent indifference to the new deep and widespread concern reflected in [the activities of] citizens' committees."[20] Citizen activity mobilized by the nuclear disarmament educational project conducted by Ground Zero in the spring of 1982 brought a million people in 650 cities and towns, 350 colleges, and 1000 high schools together to participate in meetings, lectures, films, group discussions, and demonstrations.[21]

COALITIONS FORM QUICKLY AND MAY BE TEMPORARY

The effectiveness of a coalition may be affected by its ability to form quickly around an issue or topic precipitated by a governmental action or the activity of another actor in the public policy arena. The contacts developed through previous coalitions or prior meetings greatly facilitate the formation of new groups designed to meet a specific need. The eighty coalitions recently formed by the Chamber of Commerce attests to the ease with which coalitions are formed. They need last only as long as the specific issue which brings them together lasts. If a coalition forms to pass a bottle bill, or a drunk driving law, or legislation on toxic waste disposal practices, and the legislation is enacted, the coalition may no longer be needed and may disband. The individual member-organizations may remain viable to join again in a different constellation on another (often related) issue.

COALITION FORMATION INVOLVES MIXED MOTIVES

Most successful coalitions bring together groups which may not be in general agreement but which agree on a single issue. The most effective coalitions do not require common positions on a number of issues; differences need not weaken them. An environmentalist recently pointed out that when a coalition is formed to preserve a wild river from development, some people may support it because they are avid fishermen, others because they like to canoe or kayak, still others because they don't like to see money put into a poorly conceived water project.

In fact, coalitions often make strange bedfellows. Dina Cowan and Judith Kunofsky, writing in *The Sierra Club Bulletin,* illustrate the strange bedfellows which sometimes come together. A citizen zoning issue on the ballot in Sioux Falls, South Dakota a few years ago brought together a coalition of eleven civic organizations and professional groups. In this company the Sierra Club "found itself aligned with the local Chamber of Commerce, a rare partnership of two groups that had often openly disagreed on land development and zoning practices."[22] Nevertheless, the coalition was effective. For a number of completely different reasons, the participating groups lined up to oppose zoning changes which would have resulted in poorly planned development.

Coalitions are strengthened if members agree to disagree on issues which other members may feel strongly about. Ornstein and Elder point out that the coalition to oppose the Clean Air Amendments in 1977 was greatly strengthened when the automobile unions and the industry agreed to disagree on the issues which make them "traditional enemies" and unite on their opposition to proposed emission standards.[23]

Most coalitions are built by groups whose positions lie in the middle of a spectrum. Because of ideological considerations, groups from the far left and the far right seldom engage in building coalitions with those with whom they generally disagree. The New Right has a strong aversion to any other perspective than its own. This makes it difficult if not impossible for New Right groups to engage in negotiation or compromise which typifies our political process. The result is that these groups actively disrupt the political process and openly threaten those who disagree with their positions.

Under our current political circumstances, the interest group which does not engage in coalition building with like-minded groups is not as likely to be heard in the public policy arena. The effective coalitions are the ones that make good joint use of resources, fertilize the grassroots, have an adequate coordinating mechanism, and can overlook different perspectives of other participating organizations in an effort to unite on an issue.

REFERENCES

1. "Coalitions and Associations Transform Strategy, Methods of Lobbying in Washington," *Congressional Quarterly* (January 23, 1982), pp. 119-23.
2. Salisbury, Robert H., "Interest Groups: Toward a New Understanding" in Allan J. Cigler and Burdett A. Loomis, eds, *Interest Group Politics* (Washington, D.C.: Congressional Quarterly Press, 1983), p. 368.
3. Scholzman, Kay Lehman and John T. Tierney, "More of the Same: Washington Pressure Group Activity in a Decade of Change," *The Journal of Politics* 45 (1983), pp. 351-77.
4. Langton, Stuart, *Citizen Participation in America* (Toronto: Lexington Books 1978), p. 6.
5. Additional background on the citizen participation environment can be found in chapter 1 of Joan C. Durrance, *Armed for Action: Library Response to Citizen Information Needs* (New York: Neal-Schuman Publishers, 1984).
6. Cowan, Dina and Judith Kunofsky, "Building Coalitions: The More Diverse the Members, the More Likely the Success," *Sierra Club Bulletin* 67 (September/October 1982), pp. 64-67; 94.
7. *Congressional Quarterly*, January 23, 1982, p. 123.
8. "Special Interest Lobbyists Cultivate the 'Grass Roots' to Influence Capitol Hill," *Congressional Quarterly* (September 12, 1981), pp. 1739-42.
9. Ibid., p. 1739.
10. Ibid., p. 1740.
11. Ornstein, Norman J. and Shirley Elder, *Interest Groups, Lobbying and Policymaking* (Washington, D.C.: Congressional Quarterly Press, 1978), pp. 155-185.
12. Ibid.
13. Ibid.
14. Durrance. This publication discusses citizen group activity at the national, state, and local levels. Examples of local citizen group activity are drawn from groups in Toledo, Ohio, Ann Arbor, Michigan, and Madison, Wisconsin.
15. Bromley, David G., "The Power Structure in Urban Communities," in *Contemporary Topics in Urban Sociology*, ed. by Kent B. Schwirian, et al. (Morristown, NJ: General Learning, 1977), p. 502.
16. Cowan and Kunofsky, p. 66.
17. *Congressional Quarterly*, January 23, 1982, p. 120.
18. *Encyclopedia of Associations* (Detroit: Gale Research, 1981), pp. 1291-98.
19. Ornstein and Elder, p. 39.
20. Tuchman, Barbara, "The Alternative to Arms Control," *New York Times Magazine* (April 18, 1982), p. 98.
21. *New York Times Magazine* (April 25, 1982): 4E.
22. *Sierra Club Bulletin*, p. 66.
23. Ornstein and Elder, pp. 180-84.

Creating Coalitions for a New Social Agenda

Robert Theobald

The theme of creating coalitions for the public good expresses an obvious need: we need to support the public good, and coalition building is one of the most effective means of accomplishing this. The harsh fact is, however, that there has never been greater disagreement over the definition of the public good than at the present time. We cannot create coalitions until we decide what is the public good and what kind of coalition can best serve it.

We live in a world where special interest groups try to push their own vision of the world onto the general public. Although our political process works by balancing profound disagreements, money now plays a great role in determining where the scales fall, and I think we have lost our sense of balance. The line by Yeats is apt in this context: "Things fall apart, the center cannot hold."

Effective government is, however, impossible without a center. This means that we need a centrist revolution—rather than one from the left or the right—which will recognize the interests of all citizens rather than the few. To achieve this, more and more political theorists agree, we need to move power away from central governments and back to local communities. And if we define the public good as the process of creating effective local government which serves the community, we need to ask citizens and groups to re-engage themselves in a world in which too many citizens are leaving important decisions to the state—in which citizens are "escaping from freedom," to use Eric Fromm's expressive phrase.

Both local governments and citizens in communities have been unwilling to make hard choices, but power cannot be decentralized unless we reverse this pattern. This is where coalitions fit in. Coalitions form when groups seek common cause around an overarching agenda. For instance, they have been formed to promote prohibition and to reverse it; to impose colonialism and to destroy it; to create peace through disarmament and to ensure peace through additional weaponry. Today's coalitions must address issues that are even more urgent and far-reaching.

It is my personal conviction that the impact of technology has created unprecedented social change which is tearing our culture apart. Our educational, legal, economic, political, and medical systems are in crisis. Many people believe that our educational system does not prepare us to live in today's world. Many think that we can no longer maintain a system that guarantees jobs to all who want them. And most feel profound uncertainty about the danger of nuclear war and the danger that our social contract may break down.

There is a gap between people's perceptions of what is happening and the statements made by politicians. For example, in the 1984 presidential election, all the candidates concentrated on how they would succeed in promoting maximum economic growth and maintaining full employment—no one questioned whether these were appropriate goals. The campaign highlights the difficulty we face: we can no longer strive for maximum economic growth. Rather, we must discover how to achieve optimum economic growth in a world where economic resources are dwindling and in which environmental constraints require us to live within the limits of "spaceship earth."

We not only have to move from maximum growth to optimum development, but from medical care to promoting health; from incarcerating criminals to preventing crime; from teaching only the young to learning on a life-long basis. We can no longer live with the win-lose mentality that dominates western society. That style of thinking will sooner or later lead to our destruction either through nuclear holocaust or through the destruction of our environment. But we can transform our culture from being one of competition to one of cooperation through coalition building.

Shifting social agendas is inevitably a slow and clumsy process. Indeed, there are many who claim that such a task is totally unrealistic. It is true that many cultures have had to change parts of their thinking to adapt to changing circumstances, but none has had to change their epistemology, their very way of looking at the world. But it is possible—by creating coalitions.

One agenda of new coalitions will be to find new ways of living in the information era. This presents librarians with a central role by providing coalitions with the information they need to be effective.

The barriers to libraries' offering effective support are large, however, and libraries as institutions will also have to change if they are to play their full role in supporting coalitions and effecting change.

I am quite convinced that libraries are heavily biased toward specialized, rather than generalist, literature. This bias stems directly from the Library of Congress and the Dewey Decimal systems which are designed to classify writing in terms of subject- a system of classification based on an obsolete epistemology. The universe cannot be sliced into disciplines and subdisciplines. Rather, we need to look at reality in terms of wholes and gestalts. But wholes and gestalts do not fit library classifications and books written to tie the world together rather than rip it apart vanish into library black holes. (I have experienced this again and again with computer literature searches: important information from articles and books that do not fit a disciplinary mode simply do not get retrieved.)

The critical information needs of people today goes even beyond accessibility. People—and coalitions—need help in finding information which is most relevant to their needs. People need librarians to help them with this need. Providing information *is* the natural province of the librarian. If we are to build coalitions, we can only do so if we recognize that cooperative behavior has not been our normal style. We need new styles and new skills to work with each other. Libraries can be the source of much of the knowledge we need to learn and master these skills.

We face the danger, however, that the effective librarian will be replaced by the efficient library. Although providing information is the natural province of the librarian, it could easily be lost if the tendency to see libraries as part of the overall information universe is accepted. Academic libraries, for instance, could easily be subsumed under one or another vice president in a university. And, since computer services are building more and more "help" functions into their programs, in the years to come people might find their references from the computer instead of the librarian.

Librarianship must be kept on a human scale, providing information to meet human needs. By becoming partners in coalitions, this bleak future could be prevented.

I hope that we can develop and continue the tradition of coalition building and create models which will challenge people to create a better future. I invite you to mesh your work with that of Action Linkage (Box 2240, Wickenburg, AZ 85358), an organization committed to bringing together those who see the necessity of fundamental change and want to ensure that it benefits all of society. Below is a list of publications which may form the basis of a core collection on coalition building and on the issues I have discussed.

NEWSLETTERS AND PERIODICALS

Coevolution Quarterly. Point Foundation, 27 Gate 5 Road, Sausalito, CA 94965. Theoretical and other work to promote fundamental change Quarterly.

Future Survey. 4916 St. Elmo Avenue, Bethesda, MD 20814. Monthly review of future oriented writing.

In Context. P.O. Box 30782, Seattle, WA 98103. On sustainable culture. Quarterly.

Leading Edge Bulletin. Interface Press, Box 42247, Los Angeles, CA 90042. Frontiers of social transformation. Published every three weeks.

New Options. Mark Satin, P.O. Box 19324, Washington, D.C. 20036. Reports on frontier thinking and actions. Published every three weeks.

Rain. 2270 NW Irving, Portland, OR 97210. Reports on environmental and other developments.

Tomorro's Teacher. Cathy Hainer, 235 174th Place, Bellevue, WA 98008. Future-oriented newsletter for educators, including issues, trends and classroom activities. Published five times during the school year.

Tranet. P.O. Box 567, Rangeley, ME 04970 U.S.A. Change activities throughout the world. Published quarterly.

What's Next. Monthly publication of the Congressional Clearinghouse on the Future.

INTRODUCTORY BOOKS

Beyond Despair. Robert Theobald. 1981. Seven Locks Press. A policy guide to the communications era.

An Incomplete Guide to the Future. Willis Harman. 1979. W.W. Norton. Examination of industrial society in the process of metamorphosis.

Knowing Home. Rain. 2270 NW Irving, Portland, OR 97210 U.S.A. A model for a description of one's local area.

Resource Manual for a Living Revolution. Virginia Coover et al. New Society Publishers. A study of the skills needed for social change.

Sane Alternative: A Choice of Futures. James Robertson. 1980. River Basin Publishing Company. Examination of the directions of societal change.

Seven Parables. Action Linkage, 537 Jones Street, #9175, San Francisco, CA 94102. Parables to support change.

Seven Tomorrows. Paul Hawken, James Ogilvy, Peter Schwartz. 1982. Bantam Books. Explores seven alternative futures and the choices which lead to them.

Thinking in the Future Tense. Edward Lindaman. 1978. Broadman Press. Explores the ways in which thinking needs to be changed.

BESTSELLING BOOKS

The Aquarian Conspiracy. Marilyn Ferguson. 1980. Tarcher/St. Martin's Press. Many people are involved in fundamental change.

Megatrends. John Naisbitt. 1982. Warner Books. Certain dominant trends are working which will change the world.

The Third Wave. Alvin Toffler. 1981. Bantam. Examination of the shift from the industrial era to a fundamentally changed world.

IMPORTANT BOOKS

Brittle Power. Amory Lovins and L. Hunter Lovins. 1982. Brick House Publishing. Examination of the need for renewable energy.

Evil and World Order. William Irwin Thompson. 1977. Harper and Row. World order will be changed, but not by rationalist planners.

Earth at Omega. Donald Keys, 1982. Branden. A study of the extraordinary potentials which exist at the present time.

The Global Brain. Peter Russell. 1983. J.P. Tarcher. Prospects of a leap to planetary consciousness. Worldwide transformation is not only possible, but probable.

The Next Economy. Paul Hawken. 1983. Holt, Rinehart and Winston. The world economy is being restructured from the bottom up, because of shifts in the relationship of capital, labor, energy, and new technologies.

Servant Leadership. Robert K. Greenleaf. 1977. Paulist Press. How people can lead effectively in today's conditions.

The Turning Point. Fitjof Capra. 1982. Bantam. A theoretical physicist explores transformations going on in several fields including physics, and their convergence toward a new vision of reality.

FOR CHILDREN

Creating Your Future. Kino Learning Center. Available for grades 1-3, 4-6, 7-9. Specify grade level when ordering.

Libraries and Coalition Building
Patricia Glass Schuman

The truth is, if you're going to take away the lunches of school children, the pensions of miners who've contracted black lung, the storefront legal services of the poor . . . medical care for the indigent . . . day-care centers . . . scholarships . . . transportation for the elderly and the handicapped—if you're going to eliminate people's public service-training jobs and then reduce their unemployment benefits after you've put them on the unemployment rolls, taking away their food stamps in the bargain, then I say the loss of a few poems or arias cannot matter. If you're going to close down the mental therapy centers for the veterans of Vietnam, what does it matter if our theaters go dark or our libraries close their doors?"—E. L. Doctorow

There is no easy answer to Doctorow's provocative question—his comparisons are dramatic. But, in the midst of our own individual dramas, we must not forget that these cuts are part of an extensive, systematic attack on the entire spectrum of publicly funded and managed educational, cultural, medical, legal, and social services. Public programs are being reduced, eliminated, or reorganized into oblivion and the cutbacks are neither isolated nor random. This attack has been at least partially effective because of the popular view of the public sector and its services as bureaucratic, wasteful, expensive, unproductive, and even competitive with a free market economy.

Harvard economist Robert Reich offers a compelling explanation for this shift in America's priorities. Current conventional wisdom says that permissiveness in areas like social welfare and foreign policy threaten a breakdown of our social values and our political strength. Reich's analysis[1] is based on the premise that our public philosophy has changed. A new "conservative parable" blames society's current ills on liberal excess, overspending, and weakness. The solution: "social discipline" and an "aggressive use of public power to transform the American system."

"The conservative parable," says Reich, "embodies a subtle but important distinction between two forms of social discipline—one applying to *us*, the other to *them*. *They* are the poor, the workers who demand unjustly high wages, our trading partners, Third World debtors, and the Soviets."

The public philosophy popular in the sixties and seventies no longer convinces. The liberal parable, based on altruism and conciliation, was one "of wise and generous parents who skillfully accommodate the conflicting demands of their children, help their poorer cousins, and seek conciliation with wayward relations. The modern liberal hero is a combination of Jesus and Robert Young."

While the public philosophy behind these two parables are quite different, both the conservative and liberal views are divisive and unproductive. Reich believes that a new philosophy is needed—one which:

> . . . rejects the notion—so deeply embedded within both liberal altruism and conservative pugnacity—that the central struggle of our age is over the division of a fixed quantity of global wealth. It would suggest instead the possibility of an enhanced quality of life for all, contingent upon mutual adaptation. It is crucial to understand that such an approach would be neither a matter of charity nor a ploy in a competitive struggle for survival, but an expression of a larger and more enlightened self-interest—akin to the ideal of social solidarity that modern liberalism abandoned for altruism. . . The new public philosophy would lead to policies that would embrace the new reality of interdependence. . . . "

For those of us who believe that the public good must be protected, both enlightened self-interest and recognition of this interdependence is crucial. Working together, in coalitions to further our goals, may be the only effective way we can change our current societal direction so that all of us can achieve and live in a humane, just, democratic society.

Libraries have a key role to play in this process of coalition building. Although we are surrounded by an abundance of information resources, there is a multiplicity of diverse and confusing choices for obtaining useable information when and where it is needed. Libraries are but one part of the total information spectrum which includes television, radio, newspapers, family, friends, publishers, government, databases, social service agencies, etc. However, libraries are the only institutions in our society whose underlying social *purpose* is to collect, organize, and provide access to information. In principle, if not in fact, most librarians assume an anti-censorship stance; they gear collection and public-service policies towards providing to their public free access to all sides of an issue.

Equal access to information is a natural extension of democratic principles. If information is a public good and an informed individual contributes to the benefit of society as a whole, then access to information must be guaranteed—not only in principle but in fact.

The need to know is not new. Those with the competitive edge in life are those who are best informed. What is unprecedented today is the amount of information an individual requires to negotiate his or her way through complex social and economic structures and the power of that information to determine who will do well and who will do poorly in our society.

The challenge before us is both unique and difficult. Coalitions of all interested parties at national and local levels are imperative to fight the current attempt to redefine the public good and redesign the philosophy of tax-supported public programs. Well-organized activist coalitions are essential to counteract the special interest groups, lobbyists, and PACs that are undermining the ideals we stand for.

Libraries and librarians have already experienced some success with building coalitions at national and local levels through library associations. State organizations often form successful legislative coalitions. The American Library Association has been an active partner in—and often an initiator of—coalitions on education funding, telecommunications legislation, access to government information, literacy, and similar issues. This year, ALA President, E. J. Josey initiated the Coalition for the Public Good, which has over fifty member-groups. He has also established—at the request of the ALA Council—the Coalition on Government Information to fight the restriction of access to government information.

The dramatic growth of library networks, consortia, systems, and cooperative services testifies to the benefits of collaboration around institutional boundaries.

Unfortunately, one finds few examples of active coalition building on the part of individual libraries. Some libraries do take a more active stance than others, providing basic information and referral services, routinely drawing upon unpublished, rapidly changing community data to answer questions that range from alcoholism to zoning. These libraries maintain files that deal with operational information about the community and its services; they attempt to link the needs of individuals to the appropriate service to fill those needs. Sometimes the needed information is available directly through the I&R service; more often the library functions as a basic switching center, directing people through a maze of services to the one best suited to their needs. Other libraries offer job and educational information centers. Outreach services exist in various forms in public, school, and academic libraries.

But, on the whole, libraries do not yet appear to be strongly oriented towards actively reaching out to—and working effectively with—other organized groups or institutions working on broad public-interest questions. We need to consider a much more aggressive stance.

Part of the problem is simply that most activist groups do not consider libraries as strategic access points for filling information needs. This attitude is recurrent and circular. Libraries and information services find that people are often reluctant to invest time and money to search for information in libraries because they assume that they will not find it. In part, this is because libraries have limited resources due to lack of funding. Citizens are reluctant to use and support libraries because they are not perceived as convenient, accessible, or relevant in filling information needs.

This lack of public awareness about libraries and information services, as well as misperceptions as to their credibility and effectiveness, are not only barriers to equitable access for the public, but barriers to our being recognized as effective coalition partners.

How can we overcome this perception? A reordering of our institutional priorities and the expansion of services is part of the solution. But even more essential is for libraries to seize the initiative.

A good example of how an activist stance on the part of a library might have made a difference was reported by the *Washington Post:*

> Over the past two years, parents in a housing subdivision in Morrison, CO, have watched 12 neighborhood children die of cancer, heart disease or meningitis. Another five children are battling cancer now, residents say, and there are dozens of unexplained cases of heart, brain and lung disease. The neighborhood's 5,000 residents are blaming the problem on toxic wastes and demanding government help. The Environmental Protection

Agency, after rebuffing the citizens for more than a year, recently undertook a series of surveys to search for toxic pollutants. However, the EPA has warned that it may lack the funds to do much if it turns out that the health problems stem from toxic discharges in the neighborhood. A local activist recalls bitterly that EPA officials initially told residents that they knew of no sites in the area that could pose a hazard. With one call to the U.S. Geological Survey, the citizens secured a map showing that at least five uranium mines once operated in the immediate vicinity. "You just go to the library and look it up," the local activist is quoted as saying.[3]

Obviously, it never occurred to the community activists to seek direct aid from the library. More important, it does not seem to have occurred to the local library to offer such aid.

If libraries want to participate fully in coalition building for the public good, they will have to take an active, initiating role. After all, we do have at least several "aces" to offer: *meeting space* and *information*. Recognition of these resources would make libraries a welcome partner in any coalition.

Taking an aggressive role in coalition building will be difficult because of our profession's traditional stance on the issue of "neutrality." The library parable of neutrality goes something like this: "Libraries and librarians should be neutral. Only through a neutral stance can we ensure that the concept of intellectual freedom is protected. Neutrality allows us to present information on all sides of all issues." This is a comforting mythology, but one that has not been terribly effective. To "neutralize," after all, is to make something *lose* its effect. Neutrality can obfuscate injustices and the possibilities for active contributions. Often, neutrality is not a defense of the controversial, but rather an avoidance of it. Intellectual freedom means much more than the protection of the materials on our libraries' shelves. In its broadest and most vital sense, intellectual freedom means the active promotion and protection of equal access to information as an inalienable right of all citizens.

At present, the stored knowledge contained in libraries is neither readily accessible nor heavily accessed. The use of a library requires considerable determination and sophistication. We make a grave mistake by waiting passively for others to identify a need and to perceive that the library can fill it. Access requires not only having information in our libraries, but ensuring that it is used effectively. Individuals and groups need to know they have an information need; they also need to know that the library can help them.

Our participation in coalitions can help us to work with others to promote mutually beneficial programs and at the same time heighten both the visibility and effectiveness of library service. Coalitions can enable us to build on our strengths and provide a way around existing perceptions and structures.

We librarians like to think of ourselves as problem-solvers. Institutions or groups that join coalitions usually have a problem to solve. While that problem may be shared by all members, each member of the coalition will still retain its own agenda, philosophy, structure, and constraints. Effective coalition members realize that they can retain their own character, but they also recognize that others will wish to do the same. Expected outcomes, what role each member will play, and what resources each will contribute should be agreed upon in advance; rarely will these factors be clear-cut. Constant assessments will have to be made of many questions:

- What will we get out of it?

- Will they get more than we do?

- Could we do it alone?

- What are the alternatives?

- Why is the coalition being formed: To share? To pressure? To build? To change? To influence? To improve?

- What do our prospective coalition partners stand for?

- How do they make decisions? What are their strengths and weaknesses?

- What do *we* have to put into the effort? What will *they* contribute?

These are not necessarily negative questions. The advantage of a coalition is that it can build on the *differences* between its members.

While coalitions have to appeal to the self-interest of each member, they can work effectively to confront issues on which members agree—leaving aside those on which they disagree. Coalition building first involves identifying one's allies and deciding what the minimal basis for joint action is. This may involve explaining and reshaping the parameters of the issue, leaving room for flexibility and experimentation.

This flexibility recognizes the valid differences between what an individual says, what an organization or movement says, and what the coalition says. The distinctions are not easy to make. Neither is translating our own sectarianism ("Unless our issue is the basis of the coalition we won't join it") into a broader perspective.

Negotiation and renegotiation are inherent to the coalition-building process, as is building mutual trust. "Coalitions are marriages of convenience, not overpowering romantic couplings," observes sociologist S. M. Miller. "And even with romance, and certainly with arrangements of convenience, the partners have to learn to live with each other."[4]

Recognizing this, librarians and libraries can and should be effective coalition members on many levels: as individuals, through institutions, and through their organizations. Change can and will occur if we work to join together in the fight to preserve and expand the concept of the public good.

REFERENCES

1. E. L. Doctorow, "Who Will Paint America's Guernica?", *VOYA* (February 1984), p. 319.
2. Robert B. Reich, "Toward A New Public Philosophy," *The Atlantic* (May 1985), pp. 68-79.
3. American Library Association. Washington Office. *Less Access to Less Information By and About the U.S. Government: A 1981-84 Chronology: April 1981-December 1984.* (Chicago: ALA, 1984), p. 16.
4. S. M. Miller, "Coalition Etiquette: Ground Rules for Building Coalitions," *Social Policy* (Fall, 1983), p. 19.

Ad Hoc Coalition Building: The Minnesota Experience

Suzanne H. Mahmoodi and Roger D. Sween

Librarians and information professionals are constantly assessing the needs of their patrons; they know their communities and the organizations and institutions within them, they know the activities of community groups, and they know the information resources and services available to them. As information professionals, librarians have the advantage of being aware of issues that affect their communities, and because they are knowledgeable about the informational aspects of those issues, they are in a good position to address them.

As competent planners and decision makers, librarians can be valuable in influencing public policy, especially by assuring equitable access to quality information, by developing and maintaining information and communication networks, and by encouraging those involved in any issue to use information effectively. But if they are to be effective in offering and maintaining information services within their communities, librarians must take an active role in identifying social, cultural, educational, and economic issues at whatever level they occur—organizational, community, regional, or state.

Librarians must participate in public decision making by urging their national or state professional organizations to join coalitions—and by joining coalitions themselves. They must take the initiative by forming working relationships with organizations having common goals and objectives. And because issues are constantly changing, librarians need to build coalitions which anticipate rather than react to challenges and opportunities which may not yet be recognized at the national level.

134

The following is a description of the "Minnesota Experience," an attempt to form such a working relationship, an "ad hoc coalition," first at the state level, and later to be replicated and adapted at the regional and community levels. The coalition is "ad hoc" because it was formed to meet a specific need at a specific time and will dissolve when the need is met.

IDENTIFYING THE ISSUE

In Minnesota, one of the most pressing problems is economic development. Minnesota has lost heavy industry; its number one industry, farming, is facing financial disaster and radical change. Sections of the state, particularly areas dependent on mining, have suffered high unemployment. The state is recovering from serious fiscal difficulties. The high cost of energy and high state corporate and personal taxes are perceived as causes for the poor business climate. To counteract these forces, the incumbent governor introduced an aggressive program of economic development for the state, including the creation of economic vitality task forces and councils, the development of a world trade center, and reorganizing parts of the state government structure to serve the economic development program more effectively.

Many recognized the role that libraries play in economic vitality; Leonard Inskip, associate editor of the *Minneapolis Star and Tribune*, pointed out that although libraries should be considered as part of Minnesota's economic infrastructure, the governor had not mentioned libraries in his statements on economic development programs and proposals for the state.

Library and information professionals in Minnesota realized the need to address the role of library and information services in economic development. The theme of the 1985 joint conference of the nine Minnesota professional associations representing different kinds of libraries—public, school, corporate, special, and government—was "Information: Minnesota's Natural Resource." Jerry Baldwin, Co-Chair of the conference, stated:

> Many librarians have a hard time thinking of information in the same terms as we think of petroleum, natural gas, or iron ore. Just as Minnesotans for a long time did not see our abundance of fresh water as a resource, librarians may be too close to the source and too used to dispensing 'free' information to view it as a raw resource with inherent economic value.

Historically, Minnesota has been dependent upon its natural resources—furs, forests, farmlands, ore, and lakes and rivers. A prosperous economy and vigorous society have been developed here by those who managed, and, at times, exploited these resources. But, when we look at our economy today, we see we are moving away from our dependence on these resources. As Paul Hawken put it in his recent book, *The Next Economy*, we are moving from a "massive economy" based on the extraction, distribution and manipulation of natural resources, to an "information economy" where the extraction, distribution and manipulation of information is the primary economic activity.

Nowhere, it would seem, is sufficient attention being placed on the availability and quality of the information resource itself. Nor, is there a general awareness of the need to treat information as a critical resource which must be sought out, extracted, refined, manipulated, and equitably distributed if its full value is to be realized.

Instead, we seem to be developing a myth that the computer will solve our information problems by somehow controlling the flood of information. Our policy makers do not yet understand that computers do not control information. Computers manipulate raw data in order to increase the ease and speed of creating and distributing information.

Improved computers have increased our dependence on communications, and will call for increased investment in our information infrastructure. And, just as an awareness has developed of the need for subsidized transportation to ensure equitable access to employment and services, we must develop a similar awareness among our policy makers of the importance of equitable access to information.

DEVELOPING A MECHANISM FOR ADDRESSING THE ISSUE

To develop a coalition, interested persons, financial resources, institutional support, a plan for action, and a structure for making decisions and taking action are all necessary.

For some time, the staff of the Minnesota state library agency had been considering a program to address the relationship between library services and economic development. The coordinators of the seven regional multi-type library systems asked the state library agency staff to explore methods and strategies for library professionals and those interested in library services to organize their efforts in determining and fulfilling their role in the state's economic development efforts. The opportunity to attain professional organizational support at the national level, as well as seed money for such an effort, was presented when E. J. Josey, the incoming president of the American Library Association, announced his presidential program theme: "Forging Coalitions for the Public Good." The Minnesota Library Association, which could provide interested professionals as well as support services and its organizational name, was an ALA chapter. As an ALA unit, MLA could apply for the J. Morris Jones-World Book Encyclopedia-ALA Goal Award. MLA did apply and received the $5000 award.

The president of MLA appointed an ad hoc planning group to develop the strategies and plan of action for the project, titled "Librarians as Partners in the Economic Vitality of Minnesota." He selected persons representing different types of libraries and those who were interested or involved in library services or projects related to economic development, such as the All-Association Conference. Personal attributes important to this type of group effort are the ability to understand the issue, the ability to identify key persons and organizations in economic development, the assertiveness to speak to members of the economic community, and willingness and ability to serve as spokespersons in various settings within and outside the library community. Crucial to the effort is staff support, such as a coordinator/staffperson to act upon the decisions made and to disseminate information to various interested parties. In our project, a state library agency staff member and a monitor/coordinator, hired by MLA, shared coordinating tasks.

STRATEGY FOR DEVELOPING PROFESSIONAL LINKAGES FOR ECONOMIC VITALITY IN MINNESOTA

The planning group in Minnesota adopted a strategy for fostering the development of coalitions which focused on the role of information and information professionals in planning for Minnesota's economic development and well-being, especially their efforts in job creation and the development of small business, technology, world trade, agribusiness, and healthcare delivery. Its primary purpose was to encourage those engaged in revitalizing the economy of the state to "ask us first" for quality information, to include members of our profession in planning groups and decision making, and to remember librarians and libraries any time information is required to facilitate the decision-making process. Our plan of action was as follows:

Step 1. Identify those from economic community to be involved
A. Identify the major categories of interested groups
B. Identify the networks, linkage groups, door openers

Step 2. Select a Blue Ribbon Group of those involved in economic vitality
A. Purposes
   1. To identify
      a. information needs of the economic community
      b. major issues and areas for focusing efforts
      c. resources: information, people, networks, etc.
      d. strategies and tactics for forming alliances
   2. To create awareness for the need for quality information service throughout state.
B. Criteria for selection of Blue Ribbon Group members: A person who is involved in at least three related efforts, e.g., in a coordinating group, working with the media, on a task force, making policy decisions.
C. Use of group
   1. Will meet once to identify persons and groups from economic community to be involved
   2. As resource persons, e.g., at Invitational Assembly
   3. As informal networkers by keeping them informed of efforts

Step 3. Invitational Assembly
A. Qualifications of Participants
   1. Background in some aspect of information services and/or planning for economic development and should be members of major categories of interested groups (see step 1 A & B)
   2. An investment in the topic, i.e., want to educate, to be educated, get something, be willing to give something
B. Purposes
   1. Major purposes/objectives
      a. Build further personal relationships
      b. Become aware of ongoing structural relationships
      c. Develop strategies, action plan
      d. Use information from this assembly to plan another meeting
      e. Enlarge the group of library and information professionals to become involved in effort and to expand effort to other levels, as well as at state level
   2. Secondary objectives
      a. Reports of meeting/role statements, action plan for dissemination
      b. Use process as blueprint

C. Content
1. Defining economic vitality in the state
2. Identifying the action, the decision makers, the policy makers in the focus areas
3. Defining quality information and information gathering in a focus area
4. Defining the role of library services, librarians, and libraries
5. Small group sessions on techniques for becoming involved and one discussion group on policy issues
6. Develop an action plan

Step 4. Issues Forum
A. Purposes/Objectives
1. Build further personal relationships
2. Promote new and enhance ongoing structural relationships
3. Promote and make participants aware of access to quality information offered by library and information services
B. Participants
1. Similar to those for Invitational Assembly
2. Helpful if planners, policy analysts, coordinators, directors of councils, task forces, associations, or others who can identify issues or influence policy making have some understanding of what information can do
C. Content
1. Round table discussions of major issues in area of focus
2. Developing strategies and/or organizing for action

Step 5. Regional/Local Efforts
A. Disseminate results, reports, and documents from assembly and provide opportunity for discussion
B. Introduce process for "building professional linkages for economic vitality" at regional meetings and demonstrate how it could be adapted for use at regional and local levels
C. Workshop on resources for agricultural and business enterprises
D. Present procedures and techniques for getting involved, i.e., steps 1-3

The planning group had examined a model for coalition building in the state to link educators with those concerned with the state's efforts in jobs. Steps 1, 2 and 4 above were adapted from that model. Step 3 in the education-jobs model involved setting up a working committee consisting of "doers" from the major categories identified by the Blue Ribbon Group. This committee's job was to plan and implement an issues forum, similar to step 4 above, bringing to it wide organizational support. The planning group for "Librarians as Partners in the Economic Vitality of Minnesota" saw the broadened committee as unnecessary and time-consuming and assumed the tasks of this committee itself.

After much discussion, it also decided on an invitational assembly (not in the education-jobs model) as an added step. It noted that library professionals in the state needed to be educated on the issue of economic development, their role in that development, establishing linkages with those in the "for-profit" sector, and the information needs of this targeted group. It noted, as well, that those with whom they needed to establish linkages were not necessarily persons in the top administrative positions, but rather those who have some understanding of what information can do, or who use or gather information, such as coordinators and directors of statewide task forces and councils, policy analysts, planners, etc. These persons, like librarians, would be learners as well as teachers at the assembly.

IMPLEMENTING THE STRATEGY

In studying the issue to determine the strategies to be used and how to implement them, the planning group developed a slogan to represent the purpose of its efforts: "to have librarians and library service remembered the next time." The goal was to have librarians remembered whenever members for planning and policy groups, committees, and task forces are selected, to have library resources and services remembered when information is needed, and to have libraries remembered by funding authorities at budget time.

The planning group also saw that librarians needed to know what their message to the economic community would be and that they had to have a unified message. The group therefore developed a role statement for librarians to consider adopting.

One point included in the role statement was that librarians offer access to quality information tailored to specific needs. The planning group realized that identifying the information needs of those involved in economic development, and learning their language, was vital to the success of the effort. Based on a literature search and on its meeting with the Blue Ribbon Group, the planning group began to emphasize the librarian as an information professional who could offer personalized service, and to emphasize library services rather than libraries. It also encouraged the use of terminology such as "working smarter, convenience, minimizing risk, identifying quality information," in delivering the message.

The planning group confirmed that there is a widespread lack of understanding of "what information is" and that, consequently, library service as an information service is very difficult for others to grasp. The planning group therefore requested case histories of "When Information and Libraries Made a Difference," and newspaper clippings of library services offered to those involved in economic development in the state's communities.

The planning group used the various reports and news releases of the project and the assembly, the role statement, and the action plan to keep others informed. Members of the planning group acted as spokespersons. They also considered establishing a speakers bureau and an outline of a speech that could be used by all participants. Individual planning group members, throughout the project, have used personal networking. The group then sought and received co-sponsorship for the assembly from the State Planning Agency and the World Trade Center Board.

Revising the action plan developed by the participants in the assembly and reassessing the groups' responsibilities was useful in the Minnesota experience, not only in focusing assembly participants' attention and efforts and in renewing the commitment of librarians, but also in conveying the message to others outside the field that librarians are interested in serving the economic vitality of the state and are organized to do so.

To demonstrate an information service needed by the economic community that libraries could offer, the planning group decided to develop a prototype of an online directory of organizations whose goals, services, and resources are related to economic development. The directory could provide libraries with linkages to appropriate resources. Developing an online directory service, however, requires cooperation among organizations and substantial financial support.

Librarians in Minnesota, committed to their roles as information providers and as informed members of their communities and their state, needed to address their role in Minnesota's efforts to renew the state economy. They knew they needed to join forces with other information providers, organizations, and groups in order to be heard, and to convince people to use their expertise, services, and materials. The procedure described here have been useful in building the needed "ad hoc" coalitions and professional linkages. The procedure uses three basic tactics: 1) starting with a small group, or nucleus, and bringing in, at each step, a larger number of persons from the library community and the economic community; 2) educating, coaching, and supporting each group as added; 3) disseminating information about their efforts and reporting various events and products. We are succeeding at the state level; we will concentrate our efforts next at the regional and community levels.

Librarians should consider forming an ad hoc coalition to address an issue when:

1. Addressing the issue is critical to the institution, community, region, or state of which they are a part;

2. Available library and information resources, services, and professional expertise are underutilized;

3. Information and library concerns related to the issue are not being addressed or are being addressed without librarians or other information professionals participating in making decisions;

4. Organizing, planning, and decision-making efforts do not include librarians or other information professionals.

The Coalition on Government Information

Nancy C. Kranich

The federal government is the largest collector and the largest publisher of information in the United States. Information about the government's own activities is of crucial importance to all citizens who need to make judgments about public policy. Widely accessible and low-cost government information alerts citizens to the government's policies and programs while stimulating economic, educational, scientific, and technical developments.

Since the earliest days of the Republic, the federal government has authorized numerous provisions to inform the public of government acts and to collect information essential to its operation. Recent administrative actions, however, have reversed many of these provisions and resulted in programs that disinform the public and restrict access to government information. The Reagan administration's interpretation of these provisions and its implementation of the 1980 Paperwork Reduction Act, recommendations of the Grace Commission, and agency budget cuts have significantly limited access to public documents and statistics.

In order to protect the interests of the public, librarians have become the most outspoken of groups in Washington, D.C., attacking every action which diminishes information access. To chronicle administration moves, the American Library Association (ALA) began publishing in 1981 a semi-annual report entitled "Less Access to Less Information By and About Government." A few years later, faced with restrictions on government information and threats to our system of open government, ALA council passed a resolution stating that "there should be equal and ready access to data collected, compiled, produced, and published in any format by the government of the United States."

But these actions alone could not stem the tide of events threatening the public's right to know. The alarming and continuing pattern of federal government restrictions on publications and information dissemination spurred ALA to establish the Coalition on Government Information. The coalition was organized to focus national attention on efforts to limit access to government information and to develop public awareness of and support for improvements in access to government information. The coalition's tasks are as follows:

- identify all organizations which may be concerned with limitations of access to government information and invite membership or affiliation with a coalition.

- encourage member organizations and individuals to advocate appropriate actions to improve access to government information.

- establish a clearinghouse to gather and disseminate information on barriers and limitations to access to government information from whatever source, and on efforts to promote access to government information.

- provide a national forum for exchanging ideas and programs to create public awareness of barriers to access to government information and specific examples of how barriers may affect individual Americans.

- develop a public awareness program using press releases, public service announcements, and other means to alert citizens to the importance of access to government information.

- alert concerned groups to take timely action to oppose such limitations on access to government information as transferring control of information to the private sector, which could result in de facto limitations.

ESTABLISHING THE COALITION

In 1985, the American Library Association, formed the Ad Hoc Committee to Establish a Coalition of Government Information, which has drafted goals and tasks and identified more than 200 organizations that have consistently defended citizens' rights under the First Amendment. These groups were all asked to join the coalition. The first meeting of the coalition was held on July 29, 1986, immediately preceding a public workshop on the privatization of the National Technical Information Service (NTIS).

The thirty who met on Capitol Hill represent twenty organizations with interests ranging from consumer rights, science and research, law, statistics, and libraries, to housing, journalism, and public advocacy. Participants discussed topics of particular interest to their groups and several areas of immediate concern to all, including amendments to the Freedom of Information Act, the privatization of NTIS, the pending appointment of the archivist of the United States, and the inaccessibility of many statistics collected by the federal government. They agreed to form a steering committee which would recommend a structure and operating rules for the coalition. The steering committee convened its first meeting in Washington, D.C., on October 24, 1986.

COALITION STRUCTURE

Initially, no formal structure other than a voluntary steering committee was established. No officers other than a chair were elected or appointed. Because members felt that the coalition's success depended upon its ability to act quickly when the need arose, they recommended against a rigid, cumbersome structure that might limit flexibility and timely responses to policy initiatives.

Each member of the coalition speaks on its own concerns; the coalition does not speak with a single voice on any member's behalf or for the membership at large. No consensus on issues is sought. Rather, responses from different individuals and organizations are encouraged. In this way, policy makers hear of the variety of ways people are affected by diminishing governmental information. The diversity of the coalition is its strength: it is not only a networking instrument but also an expression of wider opinion to the congressional and executive branches.

COALITION MEMBERSHIP

Membership in the coalition is open to any organization interested in the goal of ensuring equal and readily available access to government information to meet the needs of all citizens. The diversity of these groups permits the coalition to identify and communicate with a wide array of political interests, all of which make use of government information in different ways. Twenty groups were represented on short notice at the first meeting; another twenty-one showed interest in the group's activities at that time, while still others have contacted the coalition more recently. Some must receive approval to join from governing boards and councils while others are freer to make alliances without prior permission of their memberships. Participants are asked to suggest and recruit appropriate additional members while the coalition continues to expand and contact groups that have not yet responded to earlier mailings.

The following list constitutes a sampling of the organizations that have joined the coalition as of January 1, 1987:

American Association for the Advancement Of Science
American Association of University Professors
American Civil Liberties Union
American Library Association
American Society of Access Professionals
Association of Research Libraries
Association for Library and Information Science Education
Coalition for the Right to Know
Council of Professional Associations on Federal Statistics
Data Center
Fund for Open Information and Accountability
Inter-Agency Committee on Dissemination of Statistics
Librarians for Nuclear Arms Control
Medical Library Association

Metropolitan Council of the Twin Cities Area
National Association of Government Communications
National Association of Housing and Redevelopment Officials
National Committee Against Repressive Legislation
National Consumers League
National Coordinating Committee for the Promotion of History
National Newspaper Association
National Security Archive
New York Library Association
OMB Watch
People for the American Way
Project Censored
Public Citizen Open Government Project
Special Libraries Association
Women in Communications

The steering committee consists of representatives of member groups who either reside in the Washington, D.C., area or can readily attend meetings on little notice. The first chair is a member and representative of the American Library Association. Groups who volunteered to serve on the steering committee include the American Library Association, Association of Research Libraries,

National Security Archive, National Consumers League, Data Center, Council of Professional Associations on Federal Statistics, National Committee Against Repressive Legislation, and Special Libraries Association. The steering committee meets as necessary and guides the work of the coalition.

COALITION COMMUNICATIONS

Good communication is crucial to the success of the Coalition on Government Information. Members are urged to notify other participants of their concerns and suggestions and contact each other directly when an issue affects only one particular member. Each representative has a list of member organizations and their specific interests, with contact people, phone numbers, and addresses. Only when all members participate in the exchange of crucial information is the coalition's network truly effective. Initially, the American Library Association's Washington office has agreed to coordinate communications by serving as the coalition's mailing address, by editing and mailing documents, and by acting as a clearinghouse for gathering and disseminating information.

The coalition publishes an occasional newsletter which features articles contributed and signed by members. These call attention to events, trends, and governmental policies affecting the public's access to information. The newsletter is the coalition's formal communications vehicle. Articles are non-partisan and factual and are intended to inform concerned readers on issues so they can independently determine positions and necessary actions. Other means of alerting members of governmental issues of interest are through the exchange of fact sheets, testimony, articles, and other background documentation, and the semi-annual distribution of ALA's "Less Access to Less Information By and About Government."

In addition to maintaining a mailing list of interested organizations and individuals, ALA has printed a brochure describing the coalition's goals and activities. It is distributed to members and prospective members as an information and recruitment tool. It is also intended to increase the public's awareness of restrictions on government information.

COALITION FUNDING

Start-up costs for the coalition's activities were provided through a $1,000 grant from the American Library Association's

Government Documents Round Table (GODORT). This money has offset the cost of mailings, fund travel, and the coalition's newsletter and brochure. ALA has also donated a significant amount of staff time to the coalition's work. Because member groups are not equipped to contribute substantial sums indefinitely, the coalition will seek external support for some of its efforts and for staff. Not until an extensive membership list and track record are established, however, will foundations and other funding sources be eager to assist coalition programs. Until that time, the coalition relies solely on member contributions and/or subscription fees from its newsletter for its operating expenses.

FUTURE ACTIVITIES

Communications will remain the most important activity of the coalition. Through its newsletter, it will alert readers not only of important actions that require their response, but also of new publications of interest (librarians prepare bibliographies and reading lists). The coalition has also planned a speakers directory so that members can easily identify qualified individuals to address various topics. Reports of conferences, workshops, and other events will highlight public awareness activities around the country. With grant support, a videotape focusing on First Amendment and other related topics could be prepared and distributed to schools, libraries, media organizations, civic groups, and the public-at-large. Another possibility for future consideration is the creation of a congressional caucus on government information.

Given the trends over the last five years of diminishing access to information by and about government, it is unlikely that the fight to keep the public informed will end in the near future. Since 1982, one-quarter of all government documents have ceased publication, the Office of Management and Budget has consolidated its government information control powers, the trend toward contracting out and privatization of information services has accelerated, and automation has resulted in restricted access at high user-charges. The goals and tasks of the Coalition on Government Information have become increasing urgent as government information has become endangered.

In a short time, the coalition's efforts have already influenced the direction of federal information policy. Although it is difficult to determine a causal relationship between the coalition's activities and the outcomes of governmental initiatives, there has clearly been an impressive response when the coalition has encouraged comments on federal policy proposals. For example, when OMB first drafted its Circular on Management of Federal Information Resources, over 350 responses surprised that agency and caused extensive delays in revising and finally promulgating OMB Circular A-130. While the circular is still unacceptable to many of those that commented, it does include several recommendations submitted by coalition members.

Another example of effective group action is the derailing of the nomination of the archivist of the United States. A Senate Committee heard bitter attacks on the proposed appointee by more than a dozen concerned groups and decided not to act on this politically sensitive nomination before the congressional session closed. A third example of coalition impact is the substantial number of comments regarding the privatization of the National Technical Information Service, which prompted the Department of Commerce to hold a workshop to discuss alternatives and other issues arising out of comments received in response to its *Federal Register* inquiry. A final example of the success of the coalition's work is the reconsideration of a proposal to restrict public access to basic congressional documents. Rather than close both congressional document rooms and charge the public for all congressional publications, including bills, a compromise allows the public to obtain one free copy of bills, and reports or related documents from the Senate document room, which has remained open.

Without the vigilance and concern of organizations interested in preserving the public's right to know, access to government information could deteriorate even further. Through a coalition, many diverse groups can communicate the different effects of these actions on their constituents. The struggle is an uphill battle. But through the collective efforts of the Coalition on Government Information, a victory for maintaining an informed electorate is possible.

AFTERWORD
The Participants' Comments
Joseph A. Boissé and
Carla J. Stoffle

The participants in the President's Program represented every field of librarianship and many related fields as well. It is safe to say that almost every political point of view was represented in the audience. What bound participants together was, indeed, their commitment to libraries, their belief that through their educative mission, libraries are central to our society. The individuals chosen to take notes and highlight major themes and provocative ideas handed in close to one thousand pages of notes at the conclusion of the morning and afternoon sessions. The pages below represent a sampling of the comments which were on those sheets and an overview of the direction in which the discussions flowed. If one of the main objectives of the program was precisely to bring people together and to stimulate a lively exchange of views, then no one can doubt the huge success of the conference. The following synthesis bears that out.

THE PUBLIC GOOD

The task of defining the public good was approached in two quite distinct ways by the conferees. One group struggled with a philosophical definition of the concept as it applies in society generally. The other group concentrated on "the public good and the library" or "the library as a public good."

Several tables agreed that John Berry's presentation defining the public good was outstanding and set the tone for what was to follow.

There was a good deal of agreement that Samuelson's definition as reported by Berry was appropriate, i.e., the public good is a commodity whose benefits, if provided to *all* the people, come at no more cost than that needed to provide it for *one* person, and that the public good benefits everyone with no adverse effects on anyone. Others defined the public good slightly differently as a *service* whose use or consumption by an individual does not diminish its availability to any other individual. This definition anticipated a basic criticism of Samuelson's analogy of the public good as a commodity: he leaves the impression that it is a product or material which, when "used up" by one is no longer available to others.

To a great extent, the points made on the nature of the public good reflected differing views on the nature and purpose of a democratic system and its tension between the interests of the majority and the interests of the individual. One ringing dissent against Berry's thesis was that his claim that the public good "serves the entire community; protects people and property; provided service that strengthens democracy and the economy . . . is an eastern definition. Western states feel the public good is best served by minimal government, minimal regulation and that which leaves the *individual* free to do whatever he wants." As a final comment, the recorder for that group noted. "The Lone Ranger likes this definition."

Others called into question whether any definition of the public good must inevitably change with changing historical circumstances. For example, one participant commented: "The paradigm of what the public good is has now shifted due, at least in part, to supply-side economics, which is in sharp contrast to the New Deal paradigm represented by John Berry." Another pointed out that the public good *does* imply prioritization of scarce resources for worthwhile but nonetheless competing ends.

There was also concern about whether the abstract notion of the public good could be translated into concrete action. "We all agree with John Berry's definition," said one member, "but we are concerned with its implementation in the real world. There appeared to be general agreement that the biggest challenge for libraries and other institutions is to move from philosophical speculation to concrete action.

Among other, often conflicting views of the public good brought out:

- The public good is defined in its broadest sense in the U.S. Constitution and code of law, and it continues to be redefined with the growth of the country.

- The public good by its very definition must be culturally plural-istic.

- It is not important to formulate a concrete definition of the public good because the "public knows what the public good is."

- The public good is not necessarily what an individual person or segment of the public perceives as "good" for them.

- It is whatever the public decides it is at any point in time.

- There is a synergistic quality about the public good whereby the benefit to the whole of society is greater than the benefit to any single individual in society.

The recorders whose notes focused more on the library as a public good expressed some doubts about the general public's perception of the library:

- There was disagreement with Berry . . . the public does not know that libraries are for the public good.

- Libraries are taken for granted; sewers and roads are not.

Other comments suggested that we, librarians, may be our own worst enemies:

- We have not done a very good job in marketing ourselves as a public good.

- Librarians may be part of the problem in that we often act as if libraries *are not* a public good.

- We will not convince people of our worth by defensive state-ments about our worth, but by acting with our agencies to prove what we do best.

There was, however, no doubt in the participants' minds about the fact that libraries are part of the public good, and some groups expressed that belief in clear statements:

- Democracy is the highest public good the U.S. can offer its citizens; democracy is based upon an informed citizenry; an informed citizenry must have access to knowledge; the library has as its purpose the collection, organization and dissemination of knowledge; therefore, libraries foster democracy, serve the public good, and are the public good.

• Libraries eradicate information poverty so that each citizen has easy and uniform access to all areas of the community; what benefits each citizen's understanding benefits the community as a whole.

A final comment: John Berry's ideas were eloquently expressed; it's unfortunate that he was preaching to the converted.

COALITIONS

Participants were not hard-pressed to provide examples of successful coalitions. These cover every conceivable topic and exist in every state. In Wisconsin there is the Wisconsin Coalition on Intellectual Freedom, which brings together the Wisconsin Library Association, the Wisconsin Civil Liberties Union and teachers' groups together to fight the evils of censorship.

Rhode Island has the Rhode Island Coalition of Library Advocates, consisting of the League of Women Writers, Planned Parenthood, Friends of Libraries, legislators, and the arts council. The library benefits from the support of the coalition and in turn helps promote the groups through information and displays.

The Portland, Indiana Strategic Plan Task Force has brought together the public library with industry, professional groups, educators, and service clubs (a total of thirty-five groups) to work on a long-range plan to attract new industry, create jobs, and to generally improve the economic life of the community.

In a southwestern state, there is a Coalition to Save our Youth. It combines the efforts of the library with those of various youth organizations such as Scouts, YMCA, a Second Chance Group for juvenile offenders.

Libraries participated in coalitions as disparate as the Southern Louisiana Coalition to Save the Coastline, Kansas Library Resources Coalition, a Missouri Bond Issue Coalition, literacy coalitions in virtually every state in the country, "Kidsplace" in Seattle, the Family Information Resource Team in Central New York, nuclear freeze coalitions, Minority Coalition for Improved Library Service,

Health Information Sharing Network, a coalition to foster better weatherization in rural areas, a large number of human services coalitions, the Older Americans Coalition, a task force on violence against women.

These are successful coalitions, and in discussing them, participants identified several factors which accounted for that success. They pointed out that not only does every group involved in these coalitions benefit from the joint effort, but there is a broad and profound understanding of the common goal of the partners; people were convinced they were working for the common good. In many cases, the coalition effort involved both the private and public sectors. The involvement of influential community leaders helped gain attention, and diplomatic and political skills opened doors and smoothed ruffled feathers.

Interesting suggestions were made concerning new coalitions in which libraries might consider participating, including revitalized multi-type library coalitions. They included:

- forming coalitions with community groups to expand awareness of the meaning of democracy and other issues of public concern

- working closely with MADD on an alcoholism education program aimed at youth

- creating alliances between libraries and "futures" committees to enhance our long-range planning efforts

- forming coalitions with scientists and engineers to improve the distribution of scientific and technical information

- forming alliances with local non-profit organizations and acting as clearinghouses for their publications

- working closely with the advertising community to heighten awareness of libraries locally, regionally, and nationally

- getting together with RLG, OCLC, and WLN for the good of libraries nationwide.

In their discussions about coalitions, the participants also identified a variety of factors which libraries must bear in mind at all times as they work on coalition building. In some cases these factors are basic assumptions which underlie any and all coalitions; in other cases, they might be viewed as cautionary words that should not be ignored in this effort. For instance, libraries have to remain alert to the possibility that conflicts of interest or ethics may arise in the process of coalition building. We cannot forget that in any coalition, there are trade-offs—there is backscratching—that will influence our definition of the public good. It was also noted that there should be a clear reason for deciding that a particular coalition is appropriate for a library to engage in. (This suggestion was coupled with a comment that ALA sometimes gets involved in coalitions in which it has no business.) Coalitions should be formed with a specific goal in mind, participants pointed out, and when that goal is reached, they should be dissolved, i.e., coalitions should not exist just for the sake of existing. Other suggestions and cautionary comments were made:

- We need to be aware that forming coalitions can cause problems, i.e., what happens when some staff members disagree with the purposes of the coalition?

- What of the library's traditional neutrality . . . can a library claim neutrality and also participate in coalitions . . . but then isn't the idea of neutrality just another myth?

- We should beware of a possible "protect yourself" attitude which sometimes interferes with bonding together with other groups . . . we should not fear risk-taking.

The overwhelming majority of participants appeared to be convinced that libraries are already accomplishing a great deal and that more is possible. Few individuals really saw dangers in the process but some feared the possible adverse political fallout.

LIBRARY CONTRIBUTIONS TO THE ECONOMY

Few people disagreed with Gordon Ambach's statements and suggestions about the role libraries ought to play in the American economy, but they had a great deal to say about how, in their opinion, libraries currently contribute to the economic welfare of the community as well as what new initiatives libraries might make in this area. One group decided that support of entrepreneurship was the greatest economic contribution made by libraries. This same group, as well as several others, noted that one of our major problems is the lack of data available on actual economic benefits gained from libraries by individuals and/or companies. Others made the connection between the information provided by libraries and access to jobs. Many saw that good libraries serve as a magnet that helps lure new industry to many communities.

Other observations were made that underscored libraries' contributions to the economy at the local, state, and national levels; for example, many small investors rely extensively, if not exclusively, on libraries for the kinds of information they need. Libraries also provide various services to local governments that relate directly to the economic health of a community. Many ideas discussed in the groups revolved around the less direct economic contributions that libraries make, as well as their contributions to their communities' quality of life:

- Libraries provide various information services to community strategic planning groups.

- Libraries should be commended for their invaluable contribution toward personal life-long learning and for the vital role they play in the Americanization of immigrants.

- University libraries also play a role here through their fee-based information and document delivery services.

- We provide information as raw material to many writers.

- Legislators depend on libraries for information that enables them to serve their constituency.

- The children's programs in libraries contribute to the economy indirectly by making it easier for parents to be productive workers.

Although there was little disagreement that libraries ought to find a way to take a more active leadership role in addressing economic issues of current concern before those issues become overwhelming, participants also stressed that our greatest economic contribution continues to be the one-on-one link with our patrons. Here again, there were a number of cautions and reminders expressed by group members.

As one table phrased it: we must remember that our goal is not to create an improved society but to create an opportunity for personal growth which *may* in turn lead to economic growth.

Another table came to the conclusion that our success in contributing to the economy may give rise to a dilemma: the more that we demonstrate the economic benefits of libraries, the more we may be forced in the direction of establishing information as a commodity. That will set up a conflict with the public good principle, which emphasizes sharing and equity.

A very large number of tables bemoaned the fact that we do not currently have a way of accurately measuring our contribution. One group concluded that we need an economic model developed with the assistance of statisticians, sociologists, economists and demographers.

Finally, one group left us with a parting reminder: If you think education is expensive, try ignorance.

RECOMMENDATIONS FOR ALA

The annual ALA conference always gives members and non-members alike a chance to make suggestions about what the association should or should not do. Most of these discussions, however, take place in hotel lobbies and corridors or in lounges and hotel rooms. The president's program provided an opportunity for the more than one thousand participants to make written recommendations for the association based on the day's speakers and discussions. There was no hesitancy to seize the opportunity.

Several comments were made on ALA's internal fragmentation:

- One group wonders if ALA shouldn't mend itself before forming coalitions on the outside.

- ALA must speak with a unified voice; we must get our act together before we can approach other organizations.

- Fragmentation is integral to the ALA structure and this makes it even more difficult than usual to operate as an agent for change.

- ALA units should be minimized and we should form coalitions *within* the organizations.

- ALA should foster better communication between its various divisions and they should work together to develop common long-term goals.

Some comments reflected concern among the groups, who wondered whether the day's enthusiasm and effort would be wasted. They included the following:

- Don't allow the issue of coalition building to be dropped when new officers take over in ALA.

- ALA should establish an Office for Coalition Development responsible for providing resources, i.e., "how to" material on coalition building, information about successful coalitions, etc.

- Today's papers and the synthesis of the discussion sessions should be published.

- ALA should establish an association-wide, permanent commission on coalition building which would include representation from all parts of ALA.

- Provide a regular feature or column in *American Libraries* highlighting successful coalitions from the membership.

- ALA should provide state library associations or agencies with a simple program package or plan which would allow them to replicate this program.

- We suggest as a continuation of the momentum of this meeting a president's program or a smaller program next year based on the idea of YASD's NOSYAL.

- ALA should hold conferences with other occupational groups in order to extend understanding on both sides.

- The Research Office of ALA should look at how to measure the economic benefit of libraries.

There were also many recommendations made which don't fit into a group of any kind. Many of these expressed frustrations which some of the participants have experienced within ALA.

Some wanted to see a more activist association; others a less activist association. These suggestions are exemplified by the following:

- ALA should create a mission statement which focuses on librarians and not on libraries.

- Baker and Taylor (and all the exhibitions) should underwrite programs such as this rather than commit funds to social events.

- Get your act together ALA: literacy this year; senior citizens next.

- Avoid having a few people promote their own point of view and frustrate the will of the majority.

- Hire professional lobbyists.

- ALA should give up its tax-exempt status if it becomes apparent that the fear of losing it undermines the association's effectiveness.

- Fifty percent of the speakers and presenters at ALA and other library conferences should be from outside the profession.

- ALA should not alienate potential coalition members no matter what their particular political stance.

- Organize in such a way that IRS rulings won't prohibit active, visible lobbying coalitions in Washington.

- TAKE RISKS, BE BRAVE.

HIGHLIGHTS

When asked to point out the highlights of both the morning and the afternoon sessions, many commented on what might be termed technical or organizational matters. But a much larger group commented on ideas which caught their attention.

One table noted that an understanding of how coalitions are formed and work—with an emphasis on mutual compromise—was the highlight of the day. Another table was baffled, if not overwhelmed, by the difficulty they encountered in trying to define the public good.

At one table the organization representative who was present made a statement that the "library" is a great and large institution which has been relatively quiet. It is, however, an appropriate place to start the movement on the public good, and it will be able to have a great impact on our society.

The activism, or lack thereof, of ALA apparently occupied a considerable chunk of time at a number of tables. In contrast to the statement made by one group that ALA is basically a conservative organization that will not be radical at either end of the spectrum, another insisted that the association must address to what extent it can enter into PAC activities. Another group that was also absorbed with the social activism theme underscored what it perceived to be a serious problem: involving libraries in causes that are beyond library interest per se, i.e., abortion, nuclear issues, and other social issues. The fact that ALA is made up of individuals with quite basic differences of opinion was clearly reflected in these comments and others about activism.

During the day the presentations and discussions focused on the "library" in a global sense rather than on any one particular type of library. For at least one table of participants, this fact emphasized the need to build closer ties between and among libraries of all types so that indeed there will be a concept of the "library."

Several groups apparently agreed that John Berry's paper on the public good and the discussion which followed were the highlights of their day. However, one of these groups commented: Let's not delude ourselves about our commitment to providing information or about the public good; we practice censorship all the time.

The notes of the recorders included comments about each of the speakers. The one who drew the most attention, however, was Robert Theobald, and those comments blew hot and cold. One group said that he had a profound effect on their discussion late in the day and on them as individuals. Another table said simply that he gave them lots to think about. The following statements probably exemplify the two main attitudes toward his speech about as well as any:

• the second speaker (afternoon) was dynamic, but what did he really say? Was there a message or just a come-on, a sales pitch?

- Theobald's presentation raised important questions and challenged the profession to try different, non-traditional approaches to achieving social justice and the public good.

The highlight for one group was that so many concerned individuals were willing to give up an entire day of the annual conference to participate in the day-long program.

Another group felt that the intellectual stimulation and challenge was exhausting but rewarding. For others, the highlight was the active participation by such a diverse group of people, or the infectious enthusiasm that they perceived in the ballroom, or the variety of librarians represented and the expertise of the group. The international representation drew a positive response. The presence of foreign librarians offered unique opportunities to raise the concept of "public good," its definition and associated problems, to a more cosmopolitan level.

Each of the participants was seeking something in attending the session. Some wanted to explore new horizons, many were drawn by the basic participatory format, others were attracted by the major speakers. No one went away empty-handed. As one group summed up its feelings: several of us were seeking a sense of renewal and that was part of our session.

PERSONAL IMPACT

The personal impact of the program was almost as varied as there were participants. The greatest number of comments dealt with heightening the awareness of the group. People became more aware of the need to explore new directions, to try new approaches; they became aware of the commonality of interests among librarians from different types of libraries; and they become aware of the need to band with other groups in coalitions to promote common agendas.

Coalitions were the topic of the second largest group of comments reported under the "personal impact" heading. Many individuals admitted that they really did not understand coalitions very well prior to the president's program but that they were now leaving more "educated" and convinced of the need for libraries to stress coalition building. Others commented that while they already had a pretty good idea of what coalitions are and how they work, they had held, prior to the program, a rather limited view of which groups libraries might join in coalitions. The discussions in particular gave them new ideas and suggested new organizations that they will approach in the future. A few individuals apparently had not thought of some of the dangers inherent in coalition building and appreciated the opportunity to discuss these with colleagues.

Running a close third in the volume of comments were those dealing with John Berry's paper in particular and with the public good in general. Berry's presentation obviously had a strong personal impact on a very large number of the participants. It is safe to conclude from the comments that the most challenging mental exercise of the day was struggling with the search for a definition of the "public good" which would be acceptable to most of the participants at any one table. About the only point in the definition on which there was unanimous agreement was that the "public good" was a dynamic concept which changed with time and place.

The content of the program went to the heart of librarianship, it seemed to many, and inspired a vigorous new commitment to the notion that we are here to make society a better place, to enhance the quality of life of all of our fellow citizens. This commitment carries with it the need to be activist and to work toward change. Society evolves whether we, as individuals, want it to or not. Our libraries can play a significant role in charting the direction of that change. The program apparently inspired many of the participants to return to their libraries and their communities with a determination to work at that task.

Another large group of people were greatly impressed with the variety of participants. These individuals appreciated the opportunity to meet in this manner with librarians from different types of libraries. These may be the same people that one sees at state association meetings or in their own communities but they stated that this program has brought them together to discuss common issues. The program served to stress those ideas, those aspirations which tend to unite us rather than those that fragment our profession.

Perhaps the most pervasive idea expressed was this: the president's program had brought together a group of people who, apart from being librarians, saw themselves as a heterogeneous group. The opportunity to spend the day working together on these issues which are so basic to our mission proved to them that they were far more homogeneous than they had imagined.

Two comments help sum up the impact that the 1985 ALA president's program had on the participants: "Our group is having a reunion at ALA 1986. The bonding process was complete. We fought, we laughed, and we really thought." And: "Considering the importance of this program, ALA should not have scheduled anything else against it. In fact, even the exhibits should have been closed."

Notes on Contributors

Gordon M. Ambach is the President of the University of the State of New York and Commissioner of Education; also a former member of the National Commission on Libraries and Information Science. "The Library's Role in Supporting the Economic Health of the Nation" was adapted from his speech presented at the ALA Midwinter Conference.

John N. Berry III is Editor-in-Chief of *Library Journal.* "The Public Good: What Is It?" was adapted from his speech presented at the annual ALA Conference.

Fay M. Blake is a retired member of the faculty of the School of Library and Information Studies, University of California, Berkeley. "The Library's Commitment to the Public Sector" was adapted from a position paper for the President's Program.

Joseph A. Boissé is Director of Libraries, University of California, Santa Barbara. His paper, comprising the Afterword, was adapted from interviews with participants at the annual ALA Conference, in collaboration with Carla J. Stoffle.

Arthur Curley is Director of the Boston Public Library. "Towards a Broader Definition of the Public Good" was adapted from his speech presented at the ALA Midwinter Conference.

Joan C. Durrance is Assistant Professor, School of Library Science, University of Michigan. "The Effective Coalition" was adapted from her position paper for the President's Program.

William Eshelman is former President of the Scarecrow Press and a library consultant. "Serving the Public Good: Coalitions for Free Library Services" was adapted from his position paper for the President's Program.

Mary Hatwood Futrell is President of the National Education Association. "Library Services to Minorities" was adapted from her speech presented at the ALA Midwinter Conference.

Virginia Hamilton is an award-winning author of children's books. Her works include the Newbery Medal, the National Book Award, and the Coretta Scott King Award for 1983 and 1986. "The Library's Role in a Multicultural Society" was adapted from her speech presented at the annual ALA Conference.

Virginia Ann Hodgkinson is Vice-President for Research, Independent Sector. "The Public Good: The Independent Sector's Point of View" was adapted from her position paper for the President's Program.

E. J. Josey is Professor, School of Library and Information Science, the University of Pittsburgh and former President of the American Library Association. "Forging Coalitions for the Public Good" was adapted from his presidential inaugural address, June 27, 1984.

Nancy C. Kranich is Director of Public and Administrative Services, New York University Library. "The Coalition on Government Information" was commissioned for this volume.

Suzanne H. Mahmoodi is Continuing Education and Library Research Specialist, Minnesota Office of Public Libraries and Interlibrary Cooperation. "Ad Hoc Coalition Building: The Minnesota Experience" was adapted from her position paper for the President's Program in collaboration with Roger D. Sween.

Winn Newman is an attorney who specializes in labor and employment discrimination law; he is a member of the Wisconsin and Ohio Bars as well as the United States Supreme Court Bar. One of his outstanding legal victories was the landmark decision of *AFSCME* v. *State of Washington*. "Pay Equity and the Public Good" was adapted from his speech presented at the ALA Midwinter Conference.

The Hon. Major R. Owens is the first librarian to serve in Congress; he represents New York's 12th Congressional District. "The Awesome Mission of Library Leadership in America" was adapted from his speech, which he was unable to present due to illness, at the ALA Annual Conference opening general session.

Patricia Glass Schuman is President of Neal-Schuman Publishers and serves as Treasurer of the American Library Association. "Libraries and Coalition Building" was adapted from her position paper for the President's Program.

Gerald R. Shields is Assistant Dean, School of Information and Library Studies, SUNY State University of New York at Buffalo. "The Economic Impact of Libraries: A Dialogue in Search of a Coalition" was adapted from his position paper for the President's Program.

Carla Stoffle is Deputy Director of Libraries, University of Michigan. Her paper, comprising the Afterword, was adapted from interviews with participants at the annual ALA Conference in collaboration with Joseph A. Boissé.

Roger D. Sween is Continuing Education and Library Research Specialist, Minnesota Office of Public Libraries and Interlibrary Cooperation. "Ad Hoc Coalition Building: The Minnesota Experience" was adapted from his position paper for the President's Program in collaboration with Suzanne H. Mahmoodi.

Robert Theobald is an author and founder of Action Linkage. He is also the President of Participating Publishers. "Creating Coalitions for a New Social Agenda" was adapted from his speech presented at the annual ALA Conference.

Index